PRAYING AS JESUS TAUGHT US

Sixteen services reflecting on the Lord's Prayer

Susan Sayers

Kevin
Mayhew

First published in 2002 by
KEVIN MAYHEW LTD
Buxhall, Stowmarket, Suffolk IP14 3BW
E-mail: info@kevinmayhewltd.com

9 8 7 6 5 4 3 2 1 0

ISBN 1 84003 859 4
Catalogue No 1500481

Cover design by Angela Selfe
Edited by Katherine Laidler
Typesetting by Louise Selfe

Printed in Great Britain

Contents

Introduction

It is now ten years since I wrote *To Worship in Stillness*, and I am regularly asked if I could provide a similar resource of reflective liturgies. Well, here it is – a collection of sixteen liturgies, all including periods of space in which I have provided help and encouragement for using stillness as worship. There are also those liturgical conversations which people have found valuable; it is sometimes helpful to voice our thoughts in this way, corporately. There are times of intercession and singing, with suggested hymns, and passages of Scripture. Depending on the time allowed for the periods of stillness and reflection, the length of each service is flexible. It might last for less than half an hour, or be extended over several hours as part of a quiet day. The liturgies are suitable for small groups meeting at home or in church, or for larger ecumenical groups, at conferences or on retreat.

Together they form an extended reflection on the Lord's Prayer, but each service also stands on its own, as I have used the sixteen words or phrases from the prayer as headings for reflecting on different aspects of our faith. 'Our', for instance, explores and celebrates our sense of being God's community; 'Who art' gives us the opportunity to reflect on the constant presence of the living God.

Stillness and silence run counter to our culture, and many of us therefore find them unnatural and rather threatening or uncomfortable. Yet it is so often in the discipline of stillness that God can engage with our spirits and be known to us. So it seems sensible to give people some guidance and encouragement in this valuable skill of stillness. Accordingly I have provided written suggestions for how to use the times of silence. Everyone needs a copy of the service for this, as the idea is that during such times everyone can work at their own pace and as God leads them, using the written guidelines. The worship leader will need a copy of the service as shown in Part I, and the congregation copies of the service sheets from Part II.

Create a sense of 'holy space' wherever you are gathering, using the suggestions for a visual worship focus in keeping with the theme of the service. As usual, my suggestions are merely to start you thinking. The purpose of such a focus is to aid us in reflective meditation together, so nothing too elaborate or intrusive is called for. Simplicity, spaciousness and integrity would seem to be the keywords.

I have found that using quiet reflective music can also aid us in our worship. The music needs to be chosen with your particular group in mind. Develop a habit of listening to everything with your 'worship' ear, and jotting ideas down as you come across them. Film tracks are a useful source – *Gladiator* or *Schindler's List*, for example – as they are designed to be there in the background, creating atmosphere and mood. Western classical music is excellent, including some of the recent popular classics, as is music from other world cultures. Often a melody focusing on one instrument or one group of instruments is more helpful than the full orchestra. You could also use some of the beautiful Scottish or Irish folk music, and worship material from Taizé, Iona or Lee Abbey, Wellspring, Margaret Rizza or Vineyard. Don't automatically discount such sources as jazz and modern instrumental music, and nature's sounds such as ocean waves or birdsong – be open to all kinds of possibilities. The important thing is that the music aids quietness of spirit and does not interrupt reflection but helps carry it along.

In the liturgical conversations I have sometimes used the terms 'A' and 'B' so that this can refer either to men and women, or to two halves of the group, or even to individuals within it. Use whatever seems most appropriate for your particular group. With a very few noted exceptions, all hymns suggested are in *Hymns Old and New* and/or *The Source* (both published by Kevin Mayhew), as well as many other hymn books.

In writing this resource I have been constantly amazed by the richness and depth of the teaching Jesus gave his disciples on prayer. We can all benefit from coming to the familiar words in a new way, chewing them over and allowing them to nourish us and become part of us.

SUSAN SAYERS

PART I

1 Our

We reflect on our calling to be community,
bound together in the love of God

As people arrive they take a stone from a basket at the door and add it to a cairn of stones which is arranged in the worship area.

Singing 'As we are gathered, Jesus is here'

Keeping stillness During this time we will be calling to mind the routes we have travelled to be here now. Thank God for the opportunity to spend this time together as sons and daughters in the company of our heavenly Father. Now retrace your journey which has brought you to this moment. Start with the geographical route, and then move on to the spiritual route.

Leader Our heavenly Father,
as members of the Body of Christ together,

All we have come to worship you.

Leader As members one of another through your love,

All we have come to worship you.

Leader As sisters and brothers – family members,

All we have come to worship you.

Leader As your adopted sons and daughters,

All we have come to worship you.

Leader As we worship, increase our love for you.

All As we worship, increase our love for one another,
so that as your Church,
we may reflect your likeness more brightly,
and our lives may touch the world
with the love we learn at your feet.
Amen.

Singing A hymn or song of praise and thanksgiving as God's people, such as 'Now thank we all our God' or 'Praise my soul the king of heaven'

Leader How good it is to sing praises to our God.

All How pleasant and fitting to praise him.

Leader Great is our Lord and mighty in power;

All his understanding has no limit.

Leader The Lord delights in those who fear him,

All who put their hope in his unfailing love.

(From Psalm 147)

Leader Hear the prayer Jesus made for all his followers, just before he was arrested and killed. He is praying that they may all be one in God's love.

Reading John 17:13-26

This is the word of the Lord.
Thanks be to God.

Keeping stillness In your own time read over the passage you have just heard, letting it sink in that you are one of those Jesus was praying for here. So often in church we are challenged to give out, but not now. When you finish reading, know that Jesus is still praying personally for you, as for each of us, by name. You are on the receiving end of his concern and love.

Leader As God loves us, so let us love one another
A with compassion and affection;
B with understanding and acceptance;
A with encouragement in all that is godly;
B with honesty and respect.

Leader As God loves, so let us love one another.
From selfish motives and desire to take the best and highest places,
All Good Lord, set us free.

Leader From subtle discouraging and offence born of arrogance,
All Good Lord, set us free.

Leader From a critical spirit in our self-righteous conversations,
All Good Lord, set us free.

Leader From unfaithfulness in our relationships,
All Good Lord, set us free.
As God loves us, so may we love one another.
Amen.

Leader Hear this account from Luke's Gospel of the company Jesus chose.

Reading Luke 5:27-32

This is the word of the Lord.
Thanks be to God.

Keeping stillness Think over the way Jesus chose, and still chooses, the company of sinners and outcasts, so we need never feel we have sinned beyond hope of his friendship and forgiveness. Neither do we ever need to pretend we are better than we are. All our unloving, dishonest and unfaithful behaviour grieves the heart of God, but it does not make him love us less or stop longing for us to turn ourselves towards him. Let God see you now as you know you really are.

Singing   'Be still, for the presence of the Lord'

Have a time to pray for one another as you continue to worship, singing
'O let the Son of God enfold you' or 'Just as I am'.

At the end of this time of prayer, pray together:

All   Our Father in heaven,
hallowed be your name.
Your kingdom come,
your will be done on earth as in heaven.
Give us today our daily bread
and forgive us our sins
as we forgive those who sin against us.
Lead us not into temptation
but deliver us from evil.
For the kingdom, the power and the glory are yours
for ever and ever.
Amen.

Leader   The grace of the Lord Jesus Christ
be with your spirit and build you up in his love.
Amen.

2 Father

*We reflect on the parenting of God
and our relationship as children of God*

Prepare a focus of worship using an icon or a cross.

Keeping stillness As you come to the place of worship settle into a comfortable position and make your body still, relaxed but attentive. Breathe evenly. Just as our bodies provide breath for continuing life, without us often being aware of it, so God our Father gives and sustains our existence constantly; we are often simply too busy with other thoughts to notice . . . Notice now.

All All glory be to the Father
and to the Son
and to the Holy Spirit.
As it was in the beginning,
is . . . now . . .
and shall be for ever.
Amen.

Singing 'Abba Father, let me be' or 'Lead us, heavenly Father, lead us'

Leader Hear the words of the prophet Hosea speaking out God's love for his people as a parent. Although they have ignored him and turned their backs on him, and although God is hurt by them, yet still he loves them and longs to welcome them home.

Reading Hosea 11:1-11

This is the word of the Lord.
Thanks be to God.

Keeping stillness 'Abba' is a close, affectionate term for your father, such as a young child would use. And Jesus said, 'Unless you become like little children, you cannot enter the kingdom of heaven.' Think of yourself now as God's toddler, either using a loving parent/child relationship you have experienced, or receiving in God the loving parenting you long for but never knew.

Leader Abba, Father, we thank you for your parenting:
A for the gift of life and our hidden growing in the womb;
B for our birth into this earthly home.

Leader Abba, Father, we thank you for your parenting:
A for the way you look after us and care for us;
B the way you guide our tentative steps of faith and protect us from evil;

A	for the way you teach us through our experiences,
B	and listen attentively to every hesitant prayer;
A	for the way you take us by the hand and lead us,
B	and lift us high on your shoulders to carry us safely home.

Leader	Abba, Father, we thank you for your parenting:
A	for the loving and encouraging way you watch our spirits grow,
B	and give us space to learn and space to choose;
A	for the way you guide our friendships and warn us of danger;
B	hold our anger and dry our tears.

Leader	Abba, Father, we thank you for your parenting:
A	for the way you are always there for us;
B	closer than breathing and deeper than time;
A	healing our memories,
B	and calming our fears.
All	Abba, Father, we thank you for your parenting.

Singing 'The King of love my shepherd is'

Leader Hear this story which Jesus told to show us the high priority our Father gives to bringing us back into a full relationship with him.

Reading Luke 15:1-7

This is the word of the Lord.
Thanks be to God.

Keeping stillness In the knowledge of God's trustworthy parenting, bring to God your loving Father all your brothers and sisters in Christ who are in any kind of pain or distress – mental, spiritual, emotional or physical. Imagine bringing each person for whom you pray into the healing, accepting presence of the God who already knows and loves them.

All Abba, our heavenly Father,
your name is holy.
Let your kingdom come on earth as in heaven.
Let your will be done on earth as in heaven.
Give us what we need each day.
Forgive us our sins as we have forgiven others.
Do not lead us into temptation
But set us free from evil.
For the kingdom is yours alone,
power and glory are yours alone,
for ever and for ever and for ever.
Amen.

Leader   Abba, hear these prayers of your children gathered here.
We trust them with you,
knowing that you will answer
in full accordance with your loving and holy will.
As we go, may we hold on to the knowledge
that you are always our loving parent
and we your children.

All   Bless us and keep us in your love for ever.
Amen.

3 Who art

We reflect on the living presence of God,
whose name is 'I AM'

Use candles as a focus for worship. Have one candle lit, standing it on a mirror, and provide a basket of unlit candles where people come in. As they arrive they take a candle, light it and put it on the mirror before taking their place.

Singing   'To be in your presence' or 'Be still and know that I am God'

Keeping   Settle comfortably so that you can be completely still. Notice the stillness of those
stillness   around you, and of the building. Notice the steady burning of the candles, and your
              own breathing. Be still and know that God, whose name is 'I AM', is here with us
              now.

Leader   Hear this account of the way God reveals his name to Moses, a name which is related to the verb 'to be'. God is describing himself as total Being.

Reading   Exodus 3:13-15

             This is the word of the Lord.
             Thanks be to God.

Leader   In the beginning . . .
All   God . . .
Leader   In this moment now as we pray . . .
All   God . . .
Leader   In all time and out of time . . .
All   God . . .

Leader   Time-locked as we are, we struggle to understand God's ever-present and eternal nature, without beginning or ending.
All   Father, open our eyes that we may see.
Leader   The mystery of God's Being invites us to lay down our anxieties about past and future, and rest in his constancy and peace.
All   Father, open our eyes that we may see.
Leader   The knowledge of God's eternal Presence allows us access to a fresh and liberating way of living.
All   Father, open our eyes that we may see.

             Glory be to the Father
             and to the Son
             and to the Holy Spirit
             as it was in the beginning,
             is now and shall be for ever.
             Amen.

Leader Hear these words spoken by the risen ascended Christ – heard by John in his vision of heaven's eternity, and recorded by him in the book of Revelation.

Reading Revelation 21:5-7

This is the word of the Lord.
Thanks be to God.

Keeping stillness Eternity is not 'a long time' but God's 'presence' – like our 'now', but always that fresh, present moment. In this time of stillness, think over the 'new thing' which God has done in Christ. He gives us the gift of this immortal 'now' to live in here on earth, even while we live in human, mortal time. Wrap yourself in God's time-lessness and worship him.

Singing 'Great is thy faithfulness'

Leader It is God's nature to be faithful:
All in time and in eternity, God is.
Leader From before our creation to the end of all things:
All in time and eternity, God is.
Leader All knowing, all seeing, all loving:
All in time and eternity, God is.

Praying Have an open time of prayer, voicing your concerns in the presence of God, either in pairs and threes or in the whole group. Or have music playing quietly and candles available for people to light as individual prayer concerns are brought into the Eternal Presence of God.

Our Father, the Holy One,
in heavenly glory and earthly presence,
we worship you.
May all the world come to know you
and draw eternal life from your presence.
We trust you and depend on you for all our needs each day,
and for life itself.
You alone can forgive us our sins
and we ask you for the liberation of that forgiveness,
as we have set others free
by forgiving them their debts to us.
We know the power of temptation
and the importance of being watchful.
We therefore pray that we may not be led into temptation,
but that you will liberate us from the powers of evil,
without and within.
Father, we praise your name,
for you reign in power and glory
now and every now.
Blessed be God for ever.
Amen.

Leader   Safe in the everlasting arms of God,
may we live our lives set free from the fear of death.

All   May we walk through this time on earth
in the knowledge that we walk also in the courts of heaven,
through the saving love and power of Christ.

Leader   Let us bless the Lord.

All   Lord, we bless you,
and thank you, and praise you,
both with our lips and in our lives.
Amen.

4 In heaven

We reflect on God's presence in the glory of heaven

Prepare a focus for worship which expresses for you the brightness and peace of heaven — perhaps using flowers, candles and glass. Have the words 'Heaven thy throne' written at the focus point. Clear a carpeted space or provide prayer mats or hassocks so that people can kneel.

If you are able to kneel or sit on the floor, find a place to do this, so that your body is acting out your soul's longing to worship in humility the God of heaven.

Singing 'Adoramus te, Domine' (Taizé) or 'Holy, holy, holy is the Lord'

Leader Whatever is true, whatever is honourable, whatever is just, whatever is pure, whatever is pleasing, whatever is commendable, if there is any excellence and if there is anything worthy of praise, think about these things.
(Philippians 4:8)

Keeping stillness Make your body still and use your breathing to help you become attentive to the existence of heaven. As you breathe in, think of breathing God's eternal life into your body. As you breath out, think of expelling everything in you that is selfish and self-seeking. Say God's name to yourself on the in-breath and 'self' in the out-breath to remind you.

Leader Great Spirit of God,

All heaven is lit with your glory
and bathed in your love.
Heaven sings with the music of your holiness
and the depth of its silence is your peace.
Our God in heaven, though we are human
and creatures of earth,
you welcome us into this place of your dwelling,
and invite us to walk in the paths of your presence.

Leader How can anyone describe in human terms what heaven is like? As the poet T. S. Eliot said, 'words slip, slide and perish, will not stay in place . . .'. Hear these attempts by Daniel and St John the Divine to describe heaven.

Reading Daniel 7:9-14

Heaven is a little like this.
Thanks be to God.

Reading Revelation 4:1-11

Heaven is a little like this.
Thanks be to God.

Leader	Hymn writers have also tried to catch the sense of heaven. As we sing, may the harmony of words and music aid our understanding.

Singing   'O Lord my God, when I in awesome wonder' or 'My God, how wonderful you are'

Leader	Let us join together with the angels and the whole company of heaven in singing God's praise.
All	Holy, holy, holy Lord God of power and might. Heaven and earth are full of your glory. Glory be to thee, O Lord most high.

Keeping stillness   God uses our experiences and imagination to tell each of us about heaven in language we can understand. So imagine a door in a wall marked 'Heaven'. Open the door and walk through it into the place you find. Perhaps you will experience it as a beautiful garden, a vast landscape, or a place of beauty and peace you have loved on earth. Wander around this place, sensing the all-pervasive love and peace of God.

Leader	Jesus has opened up to us the possibility of sensing the life of heaven even while we walk this earth.
All	blessed be God for ever.
Women	For all that is good and holy, just and true
All	blessed be God for ever.
Men	For all that is filled with peace and love and joy
All	blessed be God for ever.
Women	For the 'thin' places where heaven and earth brush against each other and God feels specially close.
All	Blessed be God for ever.
Men	For the shining of heaven in earthly places, which takes us by surprise, and reminds us of God's presence.
All	Blessed be God for ever.
All	Our Father in heaven . . . *(pause to remind yourself of this environment of holiness)* hallowed be your name. Our Father in heaven . . . let your kingdom come and your will be done. Our Father in heaven . . . give us today our daily bread and forgive us our sins as we have forgiven those who sin against us. Our Father in heaven . . . lead us not into temptation but deliver us from evil. For the kingdom, the power and the glory are yours for ever and ever. Amen.

Singing   'Alleluia, sing to Jesus'

Leader   As in heaven, so on earth

All   may your kingdom come.

Leader   As in heaven, so on earth

All   may your glory shine in lives of love and holiness.
Amen.

5 Hallowed be thy name

*We reflect on the holiness of God, exploring some
of the names which describe his nature*

Prepare the focus for worship with some fragrance – an oil burner, a bowl of incense, a bowl of fragrant flowers or rose petals.

Singing 'O worship the Lord in the beauty of holiness' or 'May the fragrance of Jesus'

Leader Let us savour some of the names of God
and use them to worship him.

The Holy and Righteous One . . . **hallowed be your name.**
Our Rock . . . **hallowed be your name.**
The Merciful and Compassionate . . . **hallowed be your name.**
Our Healer and Provider . . . **hallowed be your name.**
My Shepherd . . . **hallowed be your name.**
Everlasting Father . . . **hallowed be your name.**
Mighty God . . . **hallowed be your name.**
Wonderful Counsellor . . . **hallowed be your name.**
Prince of Peace . . . **hallowed be your name.**
Abba . . . **hallowed be your name.**
Creator, Redeemer, Sustainer . . . **hallowed be your name.**
King of kings and Lord of lords . . . **hallowed be your name.**

Keeping stillness Take one of the names of God and stay with it a while, letting the meaning and implications of it work their way into your understanding so that you are allowing God to make himself known to you. From time to time say in the silence of your heart, 'Hallowed be your name.'

Leader May the name of God be hallowed
in the evening and the morning of each day.

A As tidal waters ebb and flow,
as mountains form and rocks are ground to sand,
may the name of God be hallowed.

B As generations are born and live and love and die,
may the name of God be hallowed.

Leader In all thoughts and feelings, memories and dreams,
may the name of God be hallowed.

A In all choices and negotiations,
may God's name be hallowed.

B In attitudes and outlooks, in crises
and in ordinary, everyday life,
may God's name be hallowed.

All Amen. May God's name be hallowed.

Singing   'Jehovah Jireh, God provides' or 'Jehovah Jireh, my provider' or 'How sweet the name of Jesus sounds'*

Leader   Hear these instructions, given by God through Moses, about the way we are to use the Holy name of God.

Reading   Exodus 20:1-7, 22-24

This is the word of the Lord.
Thanks be to God.

Leader   Hear now the words in which the Lord proclaims his name to Moses, as the replacement tablets of stone are presented on Mount Sinai.

Reading   Exodus 34:1-8

This is the word of the Lord.
Thanks be to God.

Leader   Ascribe to the Lord, O heavenly beings,
ascribe to the Lord glory and strength.

All   Ascribe to the Lord the glory of his name;
worship the Lord in holy splendour.

Leader   The voice of the Lord is over the waters;

All   the God of glory thunders,
the Lord, over mighty waters.

Leader   The voice of the Lord is powerful;

All   the voice of the Lord is full of majesty. *(Psalm 29)*

Leader   Glory be to the Father, the Son and the Holy Spirit,

All   as it was in the beginning, is now and shall be for ever.
Amen.

Keeping stillness   Remember that in heaven the angels are worshipping God. Creep into that heavenly worship now, and in reverence and humility recognise that you are in the presence of the Holy One. In your heart address God as the angels do: 'Holy. . . holy . . . holy. Holy . . . holy . . . holy. Holy . . . holy . . . holy.'

Leader   Our Father in heaven . . . hallowed be your name.

All   Our Father in heaven . . . hallowed be your name.

Leader   Let your kingdom come, on earth as in heaven.

All   Let your kingdom come, on earth as in heaven.

Leader   Let your will be done, on earth as in heaven.

* The first two hymns here may be found in *Songs and Hymns of Fellowship*

All   Let your will be done, on earth as in heaven.
Give us today our daily bread and forgive us our sins
as we forgive those who sin against us.
And do not bring us to the time of trial,
but deliver us from evil.

Leader   For the kingdom and the power and the glory are yours

All   now and for ever. Amen.

Singing   'Jesus, name above all names' or 'Immortal, invisible'

Leader   In the holy name of God
we go from this place to hallow his name
by the way we live.

All   In the holy name of God
may we live and love throughout this time on earth
and on into eternity.
Amen.

PRAYING AS JESUS TAUGHT US

6 Thy kingdom come

We reflect on our longing for God's reign in our world

Prepare a focus for worship using flags of different nations, a globe or a world map.

Singing   'Reign in me' or 'River, wash over me' or 'Jesus, remember me, when you come into your kingdom'

Keeping stillness   Think of your life and your personality as territory. If there were flags to proclaim sovereignty over this territory, which sections would be under the banner of Christ, and which would have other flags, such as 'strictly private and personal', or 'unavailable for development'?

Leader   There are places in our thinking and our loving
where we have denied access to your reign in us.
Lord, have mercy.
Lord, have mercy.

There are sections of our behaviour
where we turn your banners to face the other way.
Christ, have mercy.
Christ, have mercy.

There are pockets of resistance to your prompting,
and determination to maintain our control.
Lord, have mercy.
Lord, have mercy.

Leader   Father, give us the grace
to realign our longings with your longings,
our wills with your will,
and our vision of the kingdom with yours.

All   Father, let your kingdom come.
Reign in the whole of us
and in the whole of our life.
Amen.

Leader   In this reading from the prophet Habakkuk, hear the vision of complete saturation of the world in the glory of God.

Reading   Habakkuk 2:2-5

This is the word of the Lord.
Thanks be to God.

Leader   Now hear how the full authority of Jesus' reign over the powers of darkness is recognised by the Roman centurion, using the experience of his own temporal authority.

Reading   Matthew 8:5-13

This is the word of the Lord.
Thanks be to God.

Leader   So we pray for those in positions of authority and responsibility,
particularly wherever difficult and painful decisions have to be made.
Our Father in heaven:
let your kingdom come.

We pray for those elected to represent others
in places of government;
that your values and the example and life of Jesus
may guide their thinking and action.
Our Father in heaven:
let your kingdom come.

We pray for all monarchs
born into the responsibility of leadership.
Give them the grace and courage
to carry out their work in humility and integrity.
Our Father in heaven:
let your kingdom come.

Recognising the inherent dangers of corruption
wherever there is power,
we pray for all those with power
and influence internationally, nationally, locally
and in each home.
May they be constantly reminded of vigilance;
may they stand firm
against temptation to greed and self-indulgence,
pride, and insulation from those they serve.
Our Father in heaven:
let your kingdom come.

We pray for all who suffer
under repressive and corrupt regimes.
We stand alongside the oppressed
in their despair and silenced protest,
and pray for your justice and liberation
from all that crushes, marginalises and destroys.
Our Father in heaven:
let your kingdom come.

We thank you, heavenly Father,
for every person who has your kingdom reigning in their heart;
for all in whom your love and goodness is quietly growing;
for all whose lives you are currently transforming;
for all in whom the power of evil is being trampled underfoot.
Bless and water this growth of your kingdom.
Amen.

Singing   'The day thou gavest, Lord, is ended' (if evening), or 'Thou didst leave thy throne' or 'The King of love my shepherd is'

Keeping stillness   Think over the situations and relationships you will be part of when you leave here, and during the coming week. Welcome God to reign in those places so that, when you come to them, the ground will already be God's territory.

All   Our Father, who art in heaven,
hallowed be thy name.
Thy kingdom come.
Thy will be done on earth as it is in heaven.
Give us this day our daily bread
and forgive us our trespasses
as we forgive those who trespass against us.
Lead us not into temptation
but deliver us from evil.
For thine is the kingdom, the power and the glory
for ever and ever.
Amen.

Leader   'Do not be overcome by evil but overcome evil with good.'
All   Amen. Let God's kingdom come.

7 Thy will be done

We reflect on the need for our will to be in harmony with the will of God

As a worship focus have some bread dough on a breadboard, with some shaped rolls and small loaves, or a lump of clay with a variety of thrown pots, such as flowerpots, jugs and bowls.

Singing   'Spirit of the living God' or 'Take my life, and let it be'

Leader   Jesus said, 'Whoever does the will of my Father in heaven
is my brother and sister and mother.' *(Matthew 12:50)*

A   But what is the will of God?

B   And how are we to know?

Leader   Jesus said, 'You shall love the Lord your God
with all your heart, and with all your mind,
and with all your strength.
You shall love your neighbour as yourself.' *(Mark 12:30-31)*

All   Heavenly Father,
guide our minds and hearts as we contemplate your will.

Keeping stillness   We are using this time of silence to contemplate together, in the company of God, the love principle which underpins God's will. Read slowly the words above (Mark 12:30-31) and let God reveal to you what this means in practical terms for all of us living in the world at the moment. Think of its implications for individuals, communities, societies, nations and the Church.

Leader   Hear the words of the prophet Micah, spelling out what it means to live in tune with God's will.

Reading   Micah 6:8

This is the word of the Lord.
Thanks be to God.

Leader   Heavenly Father,
our will is so often at variance with yours,
our motives jar with your integrity,
our voiced intentions do not match with the way we actually behave.

All   Lord, have mercy on us and forgive us.

Leader   Hear these words of encouragement. It is Jesus' concern never to discard, but always to gather up and restore.

Reading   John 6:12; John 6:38-39

This is the word of the Lord.
Thanks be to God.

Leader Though we have sinned, and rejected or ignored your will,
yet you desire that nothing and no one be lost.
It is your will to search out those who have drifted far from you,
and bring them safely home.

All Lord, have mercy on us and forgive us.

Leader The leper came to Jesus and said, 'If you are willing you can make me clean.'
Jesus replied, 'I am willing; be clean.'

This is the saving word of the Lord.
Thanks be to God.

Singing 'When I look into your holiness' or 'When we walk with the Lord' or 'Will you come and follow me'

(Give each person a small piece of clay or dough.)

Keeping stillness As you shape and reshape the dough or clay in your hand, think of yourself as clay in the hands of God, the Potter, working with you in your life and circumstances, and carefully forming you. Allow yourself to trust God enough to let him make you into the person you were born to be, healing all that prevents this, and transforming all your past experiences, even the bad ones, into gifts of great value.

Press the clay or dough into the palm of your hand so that it takes on the shapes and patterns of your skin. Your life, being moulded in the palm of God's hand, will also take on his character.

(Place the pieces of clay or dough by the worship focus.)

Leader O Lord, you are our Father;
All we are the clay, and you are our potter;
we are all the work of your hand.
(Isaiah 64:8)

Leader May we learn to desire what you desire;
All your will, Lord, not ours be done.
A In every conversation and every situation,
All your will, Lord, not ours be done.
B In all the choices and opportunities,
All your will, Lord, not ours be done.
A In the rocky places where your will looks hard,
All your will, Lord, not ours be done.
B Even if sacrifices have to be made,
All your will, Lord, not ours be done.
A Even if it means shouldering a cross,
All your will, Lord, not ours be done.

Singing   'Lead us, heavenly Father, lead us' or 'Meekness and majesty' or 'Make me a channel of your peace'

All   Our Father in heaven,
hallowed be your name.
Your kingdom come.
Your will be done on earth as in heaven.
Give us today our daily bread
and forgive us our sins
as we forgive those who sin against us.
Do not bring us to the time of trial
but deliver us from evil.
For the kingdom, the power and the glory
are yours for ever and ever.
Amen.

Leader   Jesus said, 'Remember, I am with you always, to the end of the age.'
All   Thanks be to God.

8 On earth as it is in heaven

We reflect on the goodness of creation and the needs of our world

As a focus for worship arrange pictures and natural objects to remind people of the beauty of the world.

Singing   'This world you have made' or 'All things bright and beautiful' or 'O Lord my God, when I in awesome wonder'

Leader   God saw everything that he had made
All   and indeed it was very good.
A   Light and darkness,
B   water and sky,
A   dry land and vegetation,
B   sun, moon and stars,
A   sea creatures and birds,
B   animals, insects and humans.
Leader   God saw everything that he had made
All   and indeed it was very good!

Keeping stillness   Using the worship focus to help you, and the words above, spend some time sharing God's joy at the goodness of creation. Imagine seeing it all for the first time, and allow yourself to wonder and delight in the gifts of nature we mostly take for granted.

Leader   Holy . . . holy . . . holy...
All   Holy . . . holy . . . holy . . .
Lord God of hosts.
Leader   Heaven and earth are full of your glory.
All   Heaven and earth are full of your glory.
Glory be to you, O Lord most high.

Leader   Hear these words from the book of Job, where God answers Job by directing him to see the awesome holiness of God through the wonders of creation.

Reading   Job 38:1-18

This is the word of the Lord
Thanks be to God.

Leader   Father in heaven, we give you thanks and praise
All   for all the wonders of creation,
of which we ourselves are part.

A For colour and texture, light and shadow;

B for sounds, smells and tastes;

A for the laws of physics and chemistry;

B for intelligence to think with
and language to express our thoughts;

A for personalities and emotions to feel with
and respond to one another and to you;

B for the rich variety of climate, landscape and vegetation,
and all living creatures.

All Father in heaven, we give you thanks and praise.

Singing 'Praise the Lord, ye heavens adore him' or 'Confitemini Domino' or 'Great is thy faithfulness'

Keeping stillness Bring to mind the areas where there is discord between God's good creation and our stewardship of the earth we have been given to live in.

Leader Our Father

All who art in heaven,
hallowed be your name.
May your kingdom come.

Leader Father, may your will be done

All on earth as it is in heaven.

Leader Wherever greed or arrogance crash in
where angels fear to tread . . .
Father, may your will be done

All on earth as it is in heaven.

Leader Wherever destructive policies rule unchallenged . . .
Father, may your will be done

All on earth as it is in heaven.

Leader When unjust distribution of wealth
leaves some complacent and most in poverty . . .
Father, let your will be done

All on earth as it is in heaven.

Leader When resources are squandered
through short-term objectives . . .
Father, let your will be done

All on earth as it is in heaven.

Leader When war and violence, poverty and oppression
make many into homeless refugees . . .
Father, let your will be done

All on earth as it is in heaven.

Leader When knowledge races ahead of morality . . .
Father, let your will be done

All on earth as it is in heaven.

Leader   Give us this day our daily bread

All   and forgive us our trespasses
as we forgive those who trespass against us.
Lead us not into temptation
but deliver us from evil.
For thine is the kingdom, the power and the glory
for ever and ever.
Amen.

Leader   Protect us, O God, for in you we take refuge.

All   You show us the path of life.

Leader   In your presence there is fullness of joy;

All   in your right hand are pleasures for evermore.
Amen.
(Psalm 16)

9 Give us this day our daily bread

*We reflect on our dependence on God for life,
and our responsibility to share his gifts*

As a focus for worship have a loaf of bread on a breadboard.

Singing	'Guide me, O thou great Redeemer' or 'Lord of all hopefulness' or 'The Lord's my shepherd'

Leader	You, Father, are the Creator
All	and we the children of your creative love.
Leader	You, Father, are the Provider
All	and we the receivers of your gifts.
Leader	Yours, Lord, is the greatness, the splendour and the majesty.
All	For all things come from you and of your own do we give you.

Keeping stillness	Make your body still. Become aware of your breathing, and feel your pulse beating, keeping you alive. This life you have is a gift, given to you and sustained by God's love. Remind yourself of your complete dependence on God for life, and therefore all your daily needs. Wealth and temporal power lull us into thinking that we are really in control. Use this time to touch base with the deeper, hidden reality: we only exist and have free will to choose because God loves us and desires it for us. When we ask God to 'give us . . .' we are acknowledging our dependence on our Creator, and our trust in God as the Good Provider.

Leader	Hear these words of Jesus, as he teaches his followers about God's loving, daily provision.

Reading	Luke 12:22-31
	This is the word of the Lord. **Thanks be to God.**

Singing	'Nada te turbe' or 'Dear Lord and Father of mankind'

Leader	Blessed be God our Father,
All	who gives good gifts to his children.
Men	The sun shines on both unjust and just.
Women	The rain falls on both evil and good.

PRAYING AS JESUS TAUGHT US

Leader	Blessed be God our Father,
All	who gives good gifts to his children.
Women	Perfectly and finely tuned, this planet supports life in diversity and abundance.
Men	Perfectly and finely tuned, the universe is governed by laws which anchor, yet allow for development and change.
Leader	Blessed be God our Father,
All	who gives good gifts to his children.
Men	Though the gifts are taken while the Giver is ignored;
Women	though demands are made which conflict with his will;
Leader	blessed be God our Father,
All	who gives good gifts to his children.
Leader	The Lord is your keeper;
All	the Lord is your shade at your right hand.
Leader	The sun shall not strike you by day,
All	nor the moon by night.
Leader	The Lord will keep you from all evil;
All	he will keep your life.
Leader	Blessed be God our Father,
All	who gives good gifts to his children.
Leader	Let us open our hearts and minds to the gifts God wants to give us. *(From Psalm 121)*

Keeping stillness   Trusting our heavenly Father, we are going to use this space to receive from God not what we have decided we would like, but what God wishes to give us, both as individuals and as Church. We do this by faith, not sight, because the gifts may be given without any outward sign. We do it thankfully, happy to receive whatever strength or protection, healing or anointing God needs us to have, whether it matches our plans or not.

Singing   'Thank you for saving me' or 'When I feel the touch' or 'The King of Love my shepherd is'

Keeping stillness   In your imagination, gather around you those you long to know God as the giver of good gifts: those who at present do not trust him, or do not know him as he really is; those who need to know they are loved, accepted and forgiven; those who are trying to live good lives in their own strength. Imagine yourself distributing God's love to them from the huge, limitless resources of God's abundance.

All	Our Father, our loving parent, our Maker, our friend, your very name is holy.

With the angels and saints we worship you.
As you reign in heaven,
so may the kingdom of heaven extend to all the earth.
As your will is accomplished in heaven,
so may your will be done on earth.
As your created beings, we trust in your good provision.
We ask for enough to enable us to live this day
in your love and service.
We commend to you the practical needs of us all.
We ask you to forgive us,
just as we have forgiven those who have offended us in any way.
Give us your protection against evil
and guide us away from temptation
so that we do not fall into sin.
We pray these things to you alone
because the kingdom is yours,
and all power and glory are yours,
for ever and for ever.
Amen.

Leader   As God our Provider teaches us,
may we live generously, take joy in giving,
and share whatever we have with one another.

All   For in God alone is our treasure and our security.
Amen.

10 And forgive us our trespasses

We reflect on our need for forgiveness, and on God's merciful love

As a focus for worship, have a large bowl full of water, and a folded towel. Float an unlit candle on the water.

Light the candle as you say together:

All   Your light, O God, shines in the darkness
and the darkness does not quench it. *(John 1)*
Shine in our darkness, heavenly Father,
so that we may see more clearly
where our sin obstructs your love,
and denies you entrance to our lives
and residence in our hearts and minds.
Amen.

Leader   Love is patient; love is kind;
All   love is patient; love is kind;
Leader   love is not envious, or boastful or arrogant or rude.
All   love is not envious, or boastful or arrogant or rude.
Leader   It does not insist on its own way;
All   it does not insist on its own way;
Leader   it is not irritable or resentful;
All   it is not irritable or resentful;
Leader   it does not rejoice in wrongdoing, but rejoices in the truth.
All   it does not rejoice in wrongdoing, but rejoices in the truth.
Leader   It bears all things,
All   believes all things,
Leader   hopes all things,
All   endures all things.
Leader   This is the word of the Lord.
All   Thanks be to God.

(1 Corinthians 13:4-7)

Keeping stillness   Use this time to work slowly through the passage from Corinthians, substituting first the name of Jesus, and then, in the echo, your own name. You will find this will help you notice the areas of sinfulness in your living which are not 'misdemeanours' but orientation to self rather than love.

Leader   Hear Luke's account of Jesus giving the deep healing and freeing of God's forgiveness to a paralysed man.

Reading   Luke 5:17-26

This is the word of the Lord.
Thanks be to God.

Singing   'Jesus Christ, I think upon your sacrifice' or 'Jesus, remember me' or 'If we only seek peace'

Place a cross on the floor near the water.

Keeping stillness   Spend this time naming to God, your heavenly Father, the thoughts, speech, actions and missed opportunities for loving service which grieve his heart of love. Name them, neither making excuses nor shouldering blame which is not yours. Name and confess them simply out of a longing to put things right with God, and steer a new course, in the wake of his forgiveness.

Leader   Heavenly Father,
calling to mind the pain our lack of love causes you,

All   we long for your forgiveness.

Leader   Calling to mind the sadness and heartache
we have caused others,

All   we long for your forgiveness.

Leader   Calling to mind the opportunities for love and generosity
which we have missed or avoided,

All   we long for your forgiveness.

Leader   Calling to mind the righteousness we have despised
and the justice we have failed to uphold or protect,

All   we long for your forgiveness.

Leader   Lord . . . have mercy.

All   Lord . . . have mercy.

Leader   Christ . . . have mercy.

All   Christ . . . have mercy.

Leader   Lord . . . have mercy.

All   Lord . . . have mercy.

As an outward sign of this cleansing, wash your hands in the water and allow someone else to dry them. Music can be sung or played during this time.

Leader   Like water flowing in the parched desert

All   your forgiveness cleanses, refreshes and revives.

Leader   Like gentle summer rain falling after a drought

All   your forgiveness cleanses, refreshes and revives.

Leader   Like bathing or showering after a hard day at work

All   your forgiveness cleanses, refreshes and revives.

Leader   Heavenly Father,

All   it is your loving acceptance which sets us free,
lightens our hearts
and fills us with your joy.
Keep us in your love for ever,
protect us from all that is evil,
within and without,

and help us to walk in step with you,
neither dragging behind nor racing ahead
but in your close company
for the rest of our life.
Amen.

Leader May God, who alone can forgive our sin,
take from us all that is evil,
so that we can start again.
And may he refresh us daily as we travel.
Amen.

11 As we forgive those who trespass against us

*We reflect on the freedom forgiveness offers,
and our commission to set others free*

As a focus for worship, have a chain with a padlock in the open position and the key beside it.

Singing   'God forgave my sin in Jesus' name' or 'Make me a channel of your peace' or 'A new commandment'

Leader   Jesus said, 'For if you forgive others their trespasses, your heavenly Father will also forgive you, but if you do not forgive others, neither will your Father forgive your trespasses.'
(Matthew 6:14-15)

Split the group into two sections. While one half follows the Stillness exercise, the others pray for them. After a few minutes, swap roles.

Keeping stillness   This is one of the hard sayings of Jesus, but he is very clear and firm on the necessity for forgiving others. Let its significance and its implications sink in as you run your memory over your life and notice the patches where you have not yet managed to forgive completely, or where you are still holding out against forgiveness. These are bound to be the raw places where you still hurt, so you are being upheld and supported by the prayers of those around you. Don't do anything with these areas yet – just recognise and acknowledge them in Jesus' presence.

Leader   'For if you forgive others their trespasses, your heavenly Father will also forgive you, but if you do not forgive others, neither will your Father forgive your trespasses.'
(Matthew 6:14-15)

All   Father, you love and accept us,
in spite of our weak and fitful love for you.
Give us the grace to forgive others,
however much and however often
they have trespassed against us.
And wherever the hurt to us or to those we love
makes it particularly hard to forgive,
then pour into our hearts
more and more of your love and mercy
until we are able to forgive and set our enemies free.
Amen.

Leader   Hear the hard and challenging words of Jesus on the difficult task of forgiving others.

Reading   Matthew 18:21-35

This is the word of the Lord.
Thanks be to God.

Leader	God's forgiveness of us depends on our forgiveness of others. There is no way round it.
Men	No way to avoid it; no use ignoring it.
Women	No point in pretending it's done, when the bitterness still lingers.
All	God's forgiveness of us depends on our forgiveness of others.
Leader	If we say we have forgiven
Women	but the offences are stored up for use in later arguments,
All	then we still have some forgiving to do.
Leader	If we say we have forgiven
Men	but we continue to tell the story of past wrongs,
All	then we still have some forgiving to do.
Leader	If we say we have forgiven
All	but the present is still driven by the past, then we still have some forgiving to do. Father of mercy, give us the grace to forgive.

Singing	'Soften my heart, Lord' or 'Jesus, Jesus, Jesus' or 'Jesus Christ, I think upon your sacrifice'

Keeping stillness	God's grace is here in abundance for you to use. As he pours his love into your heart, be more generous in your forgiveness than you have ever been before. Reaffirm your forgiveness of situations and people you thought you had already forgiven years ago. Thank God for empowering you to forgive, setting others free.

Leader	Heavenly Father, we give you thanks and praise for the cleansing and healing of old and festering wounds; for the liberating power of forgiveness, both for others and for ourselves as we forgive.
All	Blessed be God for ever. Amen.
Leader	As Jesus teaches us, so let us pray.
All	Abba, Father, Holy One, let your kingdom and your will be accomplished here on earth as in your heaven. Provide for us our daily needs and forgive us our sin as we have forgiven those who sin against us. Do not lead us into temptation but set us free from evil. For the kingdom, all power and all glory belong to you for ever and ever. Amen.

Singing	'I'm accepted, I'm forgiven' or 'I am a new creation' or 'Lord, for the years'

Leader Will you take Christ's love out into the world?

All In the power of Christ, we will.

Leader Will you walk the way of mercy and forgiveness?

All In the life of Christ, we will.

Leader Will you build one another up in faith and love?

All With the grace of Christ, we will.
Amen.

12 Lead us not into temptation

We reflect on the power of temptation,
and our urgent need to watch and pray

As a focus for worship include a 'Danger' sign, some barbed wire and a candle.

Leader   Jesus said, 'Stay awake and pray that you may not come into the time of temptation and trial.'
(Matthew 26:41)

Singing   'Stay with me' (Taizé) or 'O Lord, hear my prayer' (Taizé) or 'Be thou my guardian and my guide'

Leader   Hear again the familiar words from Genesis, noticing the path from temptation to sin.

Reading   Genesis 4:1-10

This is the word of the Lord.
Thanks be to God.

Keeping
stillness   Think over the situations which you have found from experience are particular areas of temptation for you. They may be linked with circumstances you cannot avoid. They may be linked to physical weakness or emotional scar tissue, genes or upbringing. Recognise where you are now, not where you might be if things had been different. And know that your heavenly Father has the knowledge and power to lead you safely through the minefields of temptation. Commit yourself to his guidance, trusting him and ready to act on his leadership.

Leader   Even before we were born
All   God saw us, knew us and loved us.
Leader   Through every stage of our growing
All   God saw us, knew us and loved us.
Leader   Whenever we fought valiantly against evil,
and whenever we fell into temptation
All   God saw us, knew us and loved us.
Leader   When we lost our way and when we were oppressed,
when we were ashamed and full of guilt
All   God saw us, knew us and loved us.
Leader   For, like us, Jesus was tempted,
and understood temptation's power.
All   Like us, he was faced with difficult decisions.
Leader   The cross displays the sacrifice he made,
All   and by his wounds we are healed.

Singing	'And can it be' or 'Here is love vast as the ocean' or 'Lord Jesus, think on me'

Keeping stillness	During this time ask God to strengthen your will to remain faithful for the times of temptation ahead, and to heal those areas which make you particularly prone to temptation.

Leader Father, we thank you for your empowering.
We thank you that you know us completely,
understand our areas of weakness,
and walk with us through the valleys of darkness.

All In the shadow of your wings I will take refuge,
until the destroying storms pass by.
(Psalm 57)

Leader As we prepare ourselves by watchfulness and prayer,
we call to mind all those
who are vulnerable to temptation at the moment;
those who are cut off from their usual support and encouragement.
Father,
lead them not into temptation.

For those whose addiction is screaming;
whose anger is close to explosion;
whose debt nags and threatens;
whose desires whine.
Father,
lead them not into temptation.

We pray for those who have grown complacent
about the dangers of temptation,
or arrogant about their ability to resist.
We pray for those excited by evil and seeking it out.
Father,
lead them not into temptation.

We pray for all who entice others into temptation;
those who encourage addiction and play on people's needs;
those who profit from others' weakness or financial mistakes.
Father,
lead them not into temptation.

We pray for those who are dispirited after previous failures
and have little energy for continuing the fight against sin;
for those whose past sins stare back from the mirror
and cancel good intentions.
Father,
lead them not into temptation.

We thank you for all who work to encourage
and strengthen others in their battle against temptation;
those who make themselves available
and are ready to listen and stand alongside.
Amen.

| *Keeping stillness* | Thank God for those who have helped or encouraged you, or enabled you to avoid falling into temptation. |

All Father in heaven
whose name is holy,
may your kingdom be established on earth as in heaven.
May your will be chosen and accomplished
on earth as in heaven.
On you we depend for the gift of life and our daily sustaining.
Give us what we need and take from us our sin.
Do not lead us into temptation but set us free from evil.
We pray to you in the knowledge
that the kingdom is yours alone;
all power and glory are yours now and for ever.
Amen.

Singing 'He who would valiant be' or 'Forth in thy name, O Lord, I go' or 'Faithful One'

Leader The Lord will keep you from all evil;
All he will keep your life.
Leader The Lord will keep your going out and your coming in
All from this time on and for evermore.
Amen.
(Psalm 121)

13 But deliver us from evil

We reflect on God's power to save and rescue us

For a worship focus have white flowers, or a single lily, on a mirror, with a candle.

Singing	'O for a closer walk with God' or 'Jesus Christ, I think upon your sacrifice'

Leader	Be still.
All	Be still and know that I am God.

Keeping stillness	Just as still water reflects faithfully, so in this stillness let God's love and goodness be reflected in the still water of your soul at rest in his company.

Leader	Then I heard every creature in heaven and on earth and under the earth and in the sea, and all that is in them, singing,
All	'To the one seated on the throne and to the Lamb be blessing and honour and glory and might for ever and ever!' *(Revelation 5:13)*
Leader	As the waters cover the sea
All	so may the whole earth be filled with the glory of God.
Leader	As salt without taste is trampled underfoot
All	so may the powers of darkness be crushed beneath our feet.
Leader	May the love and goodness of God reign in every heart and mind.
All	May all that is good and lovely, faithful and true be safely gathered in, so that nothing is lost.
Leader	May we be delivered from all evil, without and within.
All	May we be set free from all that is offensive to the one true God, Father, Son and Holy Spirit.

Leader	Hear these two readings which tell of the God who saves us.

Reading	Exodus 3:4-8a

Leader	God promised to set his people free from the slavery of Egypt.
All	Blessed be God who rescues and redeems us.

Reading	Matthew 26:26-28

Leader	God promises to set his people free from the slavery of sin.
All	Blessed be God who rescues and redeems us.

Keeping stillness Let God deliver you from evil, without and within. He can free you from being a slave to any area of sin, however ingrained it feels. He can free you from the tyranny of any obsessive yearnings, destructive tendencies or buried fears. He can show you the way out of any prison of guilt, hatred or jealousy which holds you in its grip. Let him rescue you and open the doors to a new freedom.

Leader God promises to set his people free:

All free to worship him without fear all the days of their life.

Singing 'O Lord, your tenderness' or 'Thank you for saving me' or 'O the love of my Lord is the essence'

Leader Let us pray for all who suffer tyranny and oppression,
whether under corrupt government
or behind closed doors in the family home.
Father,
deliver us from evil.

We remember all for whom peace is fragile,
volatile and uneasy;
all who must be constantly vigilant
and guarded in their speech
for fear of reprisals to them or their loved ones.
Father,
deliver us from evil.

We pray for all who live in a climate of fear or ridicule;
all who are starting to believe the lies against them.
Father,
deliver us from evil.

We pray for those driven to seek asylum
far from home and family,
and all who struggle for justice
in the face of contempt or hostility.
Father,
deliver us from evil.

Keeping stillness In this space of stillness, stand alongside those who have no voice, but whose lives are crippled or blighted by the evil they face each day. Feel with the vulnerable and the desperate, and bring their pain into the presence of God.

Leader Jesus said,

All 'Come to me, all you that are weary
and are carrying heavy burdens,
and I will give you rest.

Take my yoke upon you, and learn from me;
for I am gentle and humble in heart,
and you will find rest for your souls.
For my yoke is easy, and my burden is light.'
(Matthew 11:28-29)

Leader Whenever the darkness of evil shocks us
with its terrifying power,

All give us your light to banish the dark.

Leader Whenever evil distorts truth, undermines goodness,
corrupts or destroys,

All give us the courage to stand firm in the power of love
so that we shall not be shaken.
Let the kingdom come!
Let the will of God be done!
Let evil perish!
Amen.

Singing 'We'll walk the land' or 'We are marching in the light of God' or 'Thou, whose almighty word'

Leader The Lord is faithful.

All He will strengthen us and guard us from evil.

Leader The Lord is always with us

All even to the end of time.

Leader Give thanks to the Lord for he is good.

All His steadfast love endures for ever.
Amen.

PRAYING AS JESUS TAUGHT US

14 For thine is the kingdom, the power and the glory

We reflect on getting our priorities right

As a focus for worship have a large offertory plate on which are placed symbols of wealth, power and glory, such as a wallet, a rolled degree certificate, or bunch of keys, and a glossy magazine with celebrities on it. Have the words above from the Lord's Prayer displayed beside it.

Leader   Then David blessed the Lord in the presence of all the assembly; David said:

All   Blessed are you, O Lord, the God of our ancestor Israel, for ever and ever. Yours, O Lord, are the greatness, the power, the glory, the victory, and the majesty; for all that is in the heavens and on the earth is yours; yours is the kingdom, O Lord, and you are exalted above all.

Leader   Riches and honour come from you, and you rule over all.

All   In your hand are power and might; and it is in your hand to make great and to give strength to all.

Leader   And now, our God, we give thanks to you

All   and praise your glorious name.
Amen.
(1 Chronicles 29:10-13)

Singing   'Thine be the glory' or 'Immortal, invisible' or 'You are beautiful beyond description'

Keeping stillness   Slowly and imaginatively, work your way through the words of King David's prayer, thinking of the different land, sky and seascapes of God's awesome creation, and the experience you have of God orchestrating good in the face of evil. Think of yourself as a musical instrument on which the song of God's praise is played, through the Spirit within you.

Leader   All too often we snatch at the kingdom, coveting the power and glory for ourselves.

All   But today we commit ourselves to giving God the glory.

Leader   All too often we create around us a world on which we can stamp
our will and our control.

All   But today we commit ourselves to giving God the glory.

Leader   All too often, by careful editing, we pocket the credit which rightly belongs to God.

All   But today we commit ourselves to giving God the glory.
All glory be to the one true God,
who is Father, Son and Holy Spirit;
as God was in the beginning,
is now, as we speak,
and will always be
for ever.
Amen.

Singing   'All heaven declares' or 'At the name of Jesus' or 'Holy, holy, holy'

Leader   As you hear the psalmist's words of praise, let the praises resonate in your own heart and soul, so that they become your own act of worship.

Reading   Psalm 104:1-33

This is the word of the Lord.
Thanks be to God.

Keeping stillness   Recognising that the kingdom, power and glory belong to God means relinquishing our eagerness to control, and voluntarily working co-operatively with God instead, even if the workplace and task may surprise us, and his priorities differ from our own. In this space, offer yourself to be available for the work of the kingdom on God's terms. As our desires become yoked to God's will, so we will be increasingly able to share in the work of the kingdom.

Leader   Let us pray for the Church of Christ,
that it may truly reveal God's kingdom, power
and glory on earth.
Not to us,
but to you be the glory, Lord God.

For fresh courage to look candidly at our discipleship
and welcome God's whispered advice.
Not to us,
but to you be the glory, Lord God.

For an amnesty of ambitious agendas and empire-building,
and an eagerness instead to cultivate the fruits of the Spirit.
Not to us,
but to you be the glory, Lord God.

For the grace to travel lightly, live simply
and take stewardship seriously.
Not to us,
but to you be the glory, Lord God.

For the humility to be body parts,
celebrating our membership of the worldwide Body of Christ.
Not to us,
but to you be the glory, Lord God.

For a more urgent thirst for righteousness and justice,
for fervent prayer,
and a willingness to be a part of the solution.
Not to us,
but to you be the glory, Lord God.

For closer attentiveness to God,
wider compassion, deeper faith, and greater love.
Not to us,
but to you be the glory, Lord God.
For the kingdom, the power and the glory are yours
for ever and ever.
Amen.

Keeping stillness Jesus often spoke of the hidden growth of the kingdom, starting small, like yeast or mustard seed, but with enormous potential for great effect. In this space, as we honour God, think first of yourself, and then of your church, as dough which God's yeast is in the process of transforming. Thank God for this hidden work, and pray for the yeast of the kingdom to work its way throughout the whole of the dough, so that the world can be fed.

All Holy God, Abba, Father,
reign in our lives as King.
Let our wills be at one with yours.
Give us daily bread. Take from us our sin.
Teach us to forgive.
Alert us to temptation. Guard us from evil.
To the Keeper of the kingdom we pray.
To the One with lasting power and glory we pray.
You, our Father, we worship
now and in eternity.
Amen.

Singing 'Your kingdom come, O Lord'* or 'Peace, perfect peace' or 'My heart is full of admiration'

Leader Blessed be the Lord, the God of Israel,
from everlasting to everlasting.
And let all the people say,

All 'Amen. Praise the Lord.'

* From *Many and Great* by Wild Goose Worship Group (Iona Community)

15 For ever and ever

We reflect on the nature of eternity and the eternally present

As a worship focus, have some Celtic knotwork patterns and some sand, pebbles and rock. Provide everyone with a Celtic pattern to use during the time of stillness, and invite them to take off their watches and place them among the pebbles, as a symbol of laying the concerns of time aside while we worship.

Leader	For ever and ever God is, and the things of God hold true.
All	For ever and ever the kingdom stands, sunlit with love and stretching into the distance of faithfulness.
Leader	For ever and ever the Spirit broods, breathes life and bears fruit.
All	For ever and ever God is, and the things of God hold true.
Singing	'To be in your presence' or 'Be still, for the presence of the Lord' or 'The day thou gavest, Lord, is ended'

Keeping stillness	With your finger, slowly trace round and round the knotwork pattern, thinking as you do so: 'For ever and ever God is, and the things of God hold true.' Let this pattern of movement and thinking teach your soul and settle you in the ordered love of his Being.

Leader	As time dwellers we come to visit eternity
All	and discover not length of days but a lasting presence of love.
Leader	We find not sequence
All	but orchestration. Not 'before and after'
Leader	but 'now'.
All	For ever and ever, O Lord, the kingdom is yours; for ever and ever all power belongs to you; for ever and ever your glory brightens heaven, touching earth now with the warmth of hope, and drawing us into your presence.
Leader	Hear these words written to an early Christian community and to you, now, celebrating things of lasting significance.
Reading	Colossians 1:3-20
	This is the word of the Lord. **Thanks be to God.**

Keeping stillness Use this time to consider yourself and your church as part of God's 'ever'. Think over the qualities which will last beyond death, and recognise what is only temporal. Notice any imbalance of priority in the way energy and resources are directed. Is too much time and money being spent on what is temporal, and not enough on what is eternal?

Leader Jesus said,
'Make purses for yourselves that do not wear out,
an unfailing treasure in heaven,
where no thief comes near and no moth destroys.

All 'For where your treasure is,
there your heart will be also.'

Leader St Paul wrote,
'And now faith, hope, and love abide, these three;

All 'and the greatest of these is love.'

Leader So, Father, give us the grace to seek as our priority
the kingdom of God and his righteousness.

All May we not be distracted from this calling.

Leader Father, in all our future plans and decisions

All anoint our vision with your perception;
anoint our hearing with your understanding;
anoint our activity with your direction;
that we may share in your 'ever'
as we walk through the 'now',
our lives reflecting your love
and making you known.
Amen.

Singing 'Seek ye first' or 'All I once held dear' or 'All for Jesus!'

Leader Hear the prophet Isaiah speaking out God's assurance to his people of ongoing strength and refreshment.

Reading Isaiah 40:27-31

This is the word of the Lord.
Thanks be to God.

Keeping stillness Welcome God's lasting kingdom into the different areas of your life and the life of your church. Imagine the meetings and activities, the in-tray, diary, financial reports and times of gathered prayer, committing it all to God's prioritising and in the context of God's kingdom values.

All Ever-present God, holy and loving,
your children come to pray your kingdom in.

May your reign and your will transform us all,
till heaven and earth are one.
May your feeding and forgiveness
be mirrored in our lives.
Protect us in temptation and shield us from evil.
Your kingdom lasts for ever and ever;
your power and glory never fail.
Alleluia. Amen.

Leader Heavenly Father, we give you thanks and praise
for all those through whom the message of your love
has been brought down to us.

Men For those who battled with danger and death
to keep the flame alive and deliver it on to others.

Women For those who through the generations
reflected on your love and shared what they had learnt.

Men For grandparents, parents, children and grandchildren
catching the story and passing it faithfully on.

Women For pastors and teachers,
and all whose lives have been dedicated
to the spread of your gospel and strengthening faith.

Men For all who are working now
to reach those who do not know you
and dare not trust your love.

Leader For all who have taught us by their example,
made us think, allowed us to doubt,
and loved us into the kingdom,

All heavenly Father, we give you thanks and praise.
May the story continue to be told.
May the flame of your love burn bright in our lives
and may our children's children live to praise your name.
Amen.

16 Amen

We reflect on our committed response to the call of God

Have a cross and a sheaf of flowers as the focus for worship.

Singing   'Take up your cross, he says, and follow me' or 'I, the Lord of sea and sky' or 'Dear Lord and Father of mankind'

Leader   Jesus said, 'You did not choose me but I chose you. And I appointed you to go and bear fruit, fruit that will last.' *(John 15:16)*

Keeping stillness   Let the significance of Jesus' words sink in. It is God's hand on your life which has drawn you here to be spending time in his company. It is his Spirit enabling you to pray. Keep your body still and attentive, giving God the chance to speak into your heart and mind of his love for you and his hopes for you.

Leader   Father, let your will be done in us

All   for you have the words of eternal life.

Leader   Let your love take root in us

All   for apart from you we can do nothing.

Leader   Let your kingdom grow in us

All   for your steadfast love is as high as the heavens; your faithfulness extends to the clouds.

Leader   Hear this account of Isaiah's calling and commissioning, noticing the stages of listening and new insight, repentance, cleansing and self-offering.

Reading   Isaiah 6:1-8

This is the word of the Lord.
Thanks be to God.

Keeping stillness   God never sends us anywhere without equipping us for the task. He never asks of us what we cannot do. But it is never us working in our own strength for God; it is always collaborative ministry – working with God in his strength and in step with his timing. In the stillness, ask for God's grace to understand this and act on it.

Leader   Hear now the calling and commissioning of Mary.

Reading   Luke 1:26-38

This is the word of the Lord.
Thanks be to God.

Keeping stillness	What God needed of Mary was not a total understanding of the task ahead, or of the reasons she had been chosen, but simply the willingness to say 'Yes' and go with God into the altered future, trusting him. Our 'Amen' to the Lord's Prayer is similar. It is our committed 'Yes' to God.

Singing   'May the fragrance of Jesus' or 'Let love be real' or 'Take my life, and let it be'

Leader   Let us pray for one another, that we may be firm in purpose, flexible in God's hands and filled with his love.

Pray with one another in pairs and threes for particular tasks and God's anointing for them, for areas of difficulty or confusion about direction, and for God's blessing and guidance in ongoing work and ministry.

Leader   Heavenly Father,
we think of all who pray as Jesus taught us,
and pray for them now.

Men   The very young,
who have just learnt to speak your name;

Women   the very old and frail, their lips barely moving
but their hearts full of a lifetime's trust;

Men   the sound of many voices praying as one;

Women   the tiny, scattered groups of people
praying in mountain and desert, forest and at sea;

Men   the hesitant prayers of those
who are turning back to you at last;

Women   the prayers of those imprisoned for their faith;

Men   those unaccustomed but desperate,
praying in the turmoil of disaster;

Women   those in the freshness of new faith, and full of joy.

Leader   As the planet turns, and shadows shrink and stretch
the earth is circled by the voice of prayer:

All   God's love and our response.

Leader   Like the ice of winter melting into spring,

All   let God's kingdom come!

Men   Like welcome rain on the parched and thirsty ground,

All   let God's kingdom come!

Women   Like the strong, hidden growing of roots in the earth,

All   let God's kingdom come!

Leader   Like the fullgrown wheat for the feeding of many,

All   let God's kingdom come!

Men   In hearts and households, changes and choices,

All   let God's kingdom come!

Women   In hurt and hatred, ache and anger,

All   let God's kingdom come!

All Our Father, our Parent, our great God of heaven,
let your kingdom come.
Let your will be done in us and in all your people.
Sustain us and provide for us in all our needs.
Free us from our sin through your forgiveness,
as we free others by our forgiveness.
Keep us from falling and save us from evil.
We pray in the sure knowledge
that the power and glory of your reign
lasts for ever and ever.
Amen.

Keeping
stillness   In this time give thanks to God in faith for the growth of his kingdom in every act of love and compassion throughout the world, every unselfish thought and honest transaction, every seeking after truth and justice, goodness and humility.

Leader Finally, beloved, whatever is true,
whatever is honourable, whatever is just, whatever is pure,
whatever is pleasing, whatever is commendable,
if there is any excellence
and if there is anything worthy of praise,
think about these things.

All Amen!
May our lives be transformed by the life of Christ within us.
Amen.

PART II

How to copy or download the service sheets

In order to make it as easy as possible for each person to have a copy of the service, we have set out the services in this section so that they make four-page A5 size folders. All the organising of the pages has been done for you already, and the sheets only need copying back to back and folding. The worship leader will, of course, need access to the format in Part I, which includes suggestions for a worship focus, music and so on. Space is left on the photocopiable service sheets to include the hymn or song title.

Alternatively, the text of the service sheets is available on the Kevin Mayhew website www.kevinmayhew.com/service/ so that you can download it from there and make any amendments you wish before printing and copying.

1 Our

*We reflect on our calling to be community,
bound together in the love of God*

Singing

Keeping stillness During this time we will be calling to mind the routes we have travelled to be here now. Thank God for the opportunity to spend this time together as sons and daughters in the company of our heavenly Father. Now retrace your journey which has brought you to this moment. Start with the geographical route, and then move on to the spiritual route.

Leader Our heavenly Father,
as members of the Body of Christ together,

All we have come to worship you.

Leader As members one of another through your love,

All we have come to worship you.

Leader As sisters and brothers – family members,

All we have come to worship you.

Leader As your adopted sons and daughters,

All we have come to worship you.

Keeping stillness Think over the way Jesus chose, and still chooses, the company of sinners and outcasts, so we need never feel we have sinned beyond hope of his friendship and forgiveness. Neither do we ever need to pretend we are better than we are. All our unloving, dishonest and unfaithful behaviour grieves the heart of God, but it does not make him love us less or stop longing for us to turn ourselves towards him. Let God see you now as you know you really are.

Singing

Have a time to pray for one another as you continue to worship.

At the end of this time of prayer, pray together:

All Our Father in heaven,
hallowed be your name.
Your kingdom come,
your will be done on earth as in heaven.
Give us today our daily bread
and forgive us our sins
as we forgive those who sin against us.
Lead us not into temptation
but deliver us from evil.
For the kingdom, the power and the glory are yours
for ever and ever.
Amen.

Leader The grace of the Lord Jesus Christ
be with your spirit and build you up in his love.
Amen.

Kevin Mayhew

Leader As we worship, increase our love for you.

All As we worship, increase our love for one another,
so that as your Church,
we may reflect your likeness more brightly,
and our lives may touch the world
with the love we learn at your feet.
Amen.

Singing

Leader How good it is to sing praises to our God.

All How pleasant and fitting to praise him.

Leader Great is our Lord and mighty in power;

All his understanding has no limit.

Leader The Lord delights in those who fear him,

All who put their hope in his unfailing love.

(From Psalm 147)

Leader Hear the prayer Jesus made for all his followers, just before he was arrested and killed. He is praying that they may all be one in God's love.

Reading John 17:13-26

This is the word of the Lord.
Thanks be to God.

Keeping stillness In your own time read over the passage you have just heard, letting it sink in that you are one of those Jesus was praying for here. So often in church we are challenged to give out, but not now. When you finish reading, know that Jesus is still praying personally for you, as for each of us, by name. You are on the receiving end of his concern and love.

Leader As God loves us, so let us love one another

A with compassion and affection;

B with understanding and acceptance;

A with encouragement in all that is Godly;

B with honesty and respect.

Leader As God loves, so let us love one another.

From selfish motives and desire to take the best and highest places,

All Good Lord, set us free.

Leader From subtle discouraging and offence born of arrogance,

All Good Lord, set us free.

Leader From a critical spirit in our self-righteous conversations,

All Good Lord, set us free.

Leader From unfaithfulness in our relationships,

All Good Lord, set us free.
As God loves us, so may we love one another.
Amen.

Leader Hear this account from Luke's Gospel of the company Jesus chose.

Reading Luke 5:27-32

This is the word of the Lord.
Thanks be to God.

2 Father

*We reflect on the parenting of God
and our relationship as children of God*

Do not lead us into temptation
But set us free from evil.
For the kingdom is yours alone,
power and glory are yours alone,
for ever and for ever and for ever.
Amen.

Keeping stillness   As you come to the place of worship settle into a comfortable position and make your body still, relaxed but attentive. Breathe evenly. Just as our bodies provide breath for continuing life, without us often being aware of it, so God our Father gives and sustains our existence constantly; we are often simply too busy with other thoughts to notice . . . Notice now.

Leader   Abba, hear these prayers of your children gathered here.
We trust them with you,
knowing that you will answer
in full accordance with your loving and holy will.
As we go, may we hold on to the knowledge
that you are always our loving parent
and we your children.

All   Bless us and keep us in your love for ever.
Amen.

All   All glory be to the Father
and to the Son
and to the Holy Spirit.
As it was in the beginning,
is . . . now . . . .
and shall be for ever.
Amen.

Singing

Leader   Hear the words of the prophet Hosea speaking out God's love for his people as a parent. Although they have ignored him and turned their backs on him, and although God is hurt by them, yet still he loves them and longs to welcome them home.

Reading Hosea 11:1-11

This is the word of the Lord.
Thanks be to God.

Keeping stillness 'Abba' is a close, affectionate term for your father, such as a young child would use. And Jesus said, 'Unless you become like little children you cannot enter the kingdom of heaven.' Think of yourself now as God's toddler, either using a loving parent/child relationship you have experienced, or receiving in God the loving parenting you long for but never knew.

Leader Abba, Father, we thank you for your parenting:
A for the gift of life and our hidden growing in the womb;
B for our birth into this earthly home.

Leader Abba, Father, we thank you for your parenting:
A for the way you look after us and care for us;
B the way you guide our tentative steps of faith and protect us from evil;
A for the way you teach us through our experiences,
B and listen attentively to every hesitant prayer;
A for the way you take us by the hand and lead us,
B and lift us high on your shoulders to carry us safely home.

Leader Abba, Father, we thank you for your parenting:
A for the loving and encouraging way you watch our spirits grow,
B and give us space to learn and space to choose;
A for the way you guide our friendships and warn us of danger;
B hold our anger and dry our tears.

Leader Abba, Father, we thank you for your parenting:
A for the way you are always there for us;
B closer than breathing and deeper than time;
A healing our memories,
B and calming our fears.
All Abba, Father, we thank you for your parenting.

Singing

Leader Hear this story which Jesus told to show us the high priority our Father gives to bringing us back into a full relationship with him.

Reading Luke 15:1-7

This is the word of the Lord.
Thanks be to God.

Keeping stillness In the knowledge of God's trustworthy parenting, bring to God your loving Father all your brothers and sisters in Christ who are in any kind of pain or distress – mental, spiritual, emotional or physical. Imagine bringing each person for whom you pray into the healing, accepting presence of the God who already knows and loves them.

All Abba, our heavenly Father,
your name is holy.
Let your kingdom come on earth as in heaven.
Let your will be done on earth as in heaven.
Give us what we need each day.
Forgive us our sins as we have forgiven others.

3 Who art

We reflect on the living presence of God, whose name is 'I AM'

Singing

Keeping stillness Settle comfortably so that you can be completely still. Notice the stillness of those around you, and of the building. Notice the steady burning of the candles, and your own breathing. Be still and know that God, whose name is 'I AM', is here with us now.

Leader Hear this account of the way God reveals his name to Moses, a name which is related to the verb 'to be'. God is describing himself as total Being.

Reading Exodus 3:13-15

This is the word of the Lord.
Thanks be to God.

Leader In the beginning . . . .
All God . . . .
Leader In this moment now as we pray . . . .
All God . . . .
Leader In all time and out of time . . . .
All God . . . .

Leader   Time-locked as we are, we struggle to understand God's ever-present and eternal nature, without beginning or ending.

All   Father, open our eyes that we may see.

Leader   The mystery of God's Being invites us to lay down our anxieties about past and future, and rest in his constancy and peace.

All   Father, open our eyes that we may see.

Leader   The knowledge of God's eternal Presence allows us access to a fresh and liberating way of living.

All   Father, open our eyes that we may see.

> Glory be to the Father
> and to the Son
> and to the Holy Spirit
> as it was in the beginning,
> is now and shall be for ever.
> Amen.

Leader   Hear these words spoken by the risen ascended Christ – heard by John in his vision of heaven's eternity, and recorded by him in the book of Revelation.

Reading   Revelation 21:5–7

This is the word of the Lord.
Thanks be to God.

Keeping stillness   Eternity is not 'a long time' but God's 'presence' – like our 'now', but always that fresh, present moment. In this time of stillness, think over the 'new thing' which God has done in Christ. He gives us the gift of this immortal 'now' to live in here on earth, even while we live in human, mortal time. Wrap yourself in God's timelessness and worship him.

Singing

Leader   It is God's nature to be faithful:

All   in time and in eternity, God is.

Leader   From before our creation to the end of all things:

All   in time and eternity, God is.

Leader   All knowing, all seeing, all loving:

All   in time and eternity, God is.

Praying   Have an open time of prayer, voicing your concerns in the presence of God, either in pairs and threes or in the whole group. Or you may prefer to have music playing quietly and candles available for people to light as individual prayer concerns are brought into the Eternal Presence of God.

Leader   Safe in the everlasting arms of God, may we live our lives set free from the fear of death.

All   May we walk through this time on earth in the knowledge that we walk also in the courts of heaven, through the saving love and power of Christ.

Leader   Let us bless the Lord.

All   Lord, we bless you, and thank you, and praise you, both with our lips and in our lives. Amen.

Singing

Leader As in heaven, so on earth

All may your kingdom come.

Leader As in heaven, so on earth

All may your glory shine in lives of love and holiness.
Amen.

4 In heaven

We reflect on God's presence in the glory of heaven

Singing

Leader Whatever is true, whatever is honourable, whatever is just, whatever is pure, whatever is pleasing, whatever is commendable, if there is any excellence and if there is anything worthy of praise, think about these things.
(Philippians 4:8)

Keeping stillness Make your body still and use your breathing to help you become attentive to the existence of heaven. As you breathe in, think of breathing God's eternal life into your body. As you breath out, think of expelling everything in you that is selfish and self-seeking. Say God's name to yourself on the in-breath and 'self' in the out-breath to remind you.

Leader Great Spirit of God,

All heaven is lit with your glory
and bathed in your love.
Heaven sings with the music of your holiness
and the depth of its silence is your peace.
Our God in heaven, though we are human
and creatures of earth,
you welcome us into this place of your dwelling,
and invite us to walk in the paths of your presence.

Kevin Mayhew

Leader How can anyone describe in human terms what heaven is like? As the poet T. S. Eliot said, 'words slip, slide and perish, will not stay in place . . .'. Hear these attempts by Daniel and St John the Divine to describe heaven.

Reading Daniel 7:9-14

Heaven is a little like this.
Thanks be to God.

Reading Revelation 4:1-11

Heaven is a little like this.
Thanks be to God.

Leader Hymn writers have also tried to catch the sense of heaven. As we sing, may the harmony of words and music aid our understanding.

Singing

Leader Let us join together with the angels and the whole company of heaven in singing God's praise.

All Holy, holy, holy Lord
God of power and might.
Heaven and earth are full of your glory.
Glory be to thee, O Lord most high.

Keeping stillness God uses our experiences and imagination to tell each of us about heaven in language we can understand. So imagine a door in a wall marked 'Heaven'. Open the door and walk through it into the place you find. Perhaps you will experience it as a

beautiful garden, a vast landscape, or a place of beauty and peace you have loved on earth. Wander around this place, sensing the all-pervasive love and peace of God.

Leader Jesus has opened up to us the possibility of sensing the life of heaven even while we walk this earth.

All Blessed be God for ever.

Women For all that is good and holy, just and true

All blessed be God for ever.

Men For all that is filled with peace and love and joy

All blessed be God for ever.

Women For the 'thin' places where heaven and earth brush against each other and God feels specially close.

All Blessed be God for ever.

Men For the shining of heaven in earthly places, which takes us by surprise, and reminds us of God's presence.

All Blessed be God for ever.

All Our Father in heaven . . .
(pause to remind yourself of this environment of holiness)
hallowed be your name.
Our Father in heaven . . . .
let your kingdom come and your will be done.
Our Father in heaven . . . .
give us today our daily bread
and forgive us our sins
as we have forgiven those who sin against us.
Our Father in heaven . . . .
lead us not into temptation but deliver us from evil.
For the kingdom, the power and the glory are yours
for ever and ever.
Amen.

Leader For the kingdom and the power and the glory are yours

All now and for ever. Amen.

Singing

5 Hallowed be thy name

We reflect on the holiness of God, exploring some of the names which describe his nature

Singing

Leader In the holy name of God
we go from this place to hallow his name
by the way we live.

Leader Let us savour some of the names of God
and use them to worship him.

All In the holy name of God
may we live and love throughout this time on earth
and on into eternity.
Amen.

The Holy and Righteous One . . . **hallowed be your name.**
Our Rock . . . **hallowed be your name.**
The Merciful and Compassionate . . . **hallowed be your name.**
Our Healer and Provider . . . **hallowed be your name.**
My Shepherd . . . **hallowed be your name.**
Everlasting Father . . . **hallowed be your name.**
Mighty God . . . **hallowed be your name.**
Wonderful Counsellor . . . **hallowed be your name.**
Prince of Peace . . . **hallowed be your name.**
Abba . . . **hallowed be your name.**
Creator, Redeemer, Sustainer . . . **hallowed be your name.**
King of kings and Lord of lords . . . **hallowed be your name.**

Keeping stillness Take one of the names of God and stay with it a while, letting the meaning and implications of it work their way into your understanding so that you are allowing God to make himself known to you. From time to time say in the silence of your heart, 'Hallowed be your name.'

Kevin Mayhew

Leader May the name of God be hallowed
in the evening and the morning of each day.

A As tidal waters ebb and flow,
as mountains form and rocks are ground to sand,
may the name of God be hallowed.

B As generations are born and live and love and die,
may the name of God be hallowed.

Leader In all thoughts and feelings, memories and dreams,
may the name of God be hallowed.

A In all choices and negotiations,
may God's name be hallowed.

B In attitudes and outlooks, in crises
and in ordinary, everyday life,
may God's name be hallowed.

All Amen. May God's name be hallowed.

Singing

Leader Hear these instructions, given by God through Moses, about the way we are to use the Holy name of God.

Reading Exodus 20:1-7, 22-24

This is the word of the Lord.
Thanks be to God.

Leader Hear now the words in which the Lord proclaims his name to Moses, as the replacement tablets of stone are presented on Mount Sinai.

Reading Exodus 34:1-8

This is the word of the Lord.
Thanks be to God.

Leader Ascribe to the Lord, O heavenly beings,
ascribe to the Lord glory and strength.

All Ascribe to the Lord the glory of his name;
worship the Lord in holy splendour.

Leader The voice of the Lord is over the waters;

All the God of glory thunders,
the Lord, over mighty waters.

Leader The voice of the Lord is powerful;

All the voice of the Lord is full of majesty. *(Psalm 29)*

Leader Glory be to the Father, the Son and the Holy Spirit,

All as it was in the beginning, is now and shall be for ever.
Amen.

Keeping stillness Remember that in heaven the angels are worshipping God. Creep into that heavenly worship now, and in reverence and humility recognise that you are in the presence of the Holy One. In your heart address God as the angels do: 'Holy . . . holy . . . holy. Holy . . . holy . . . holy. Holy . . . holy . . . holy.'

Leader Our Father in heaven . . . hallowed be your name.

All Our Father in heaven . . . hallowed be your name.

Leader Let your kingdom come, on earth as in heaven.

All Let your kingdom come, on earth as in heaven.

Leader Let your will be done, on earth as in heaven.

All Let your will be done, on earth as in heaven.
Give us today our daily bread and forgive us our sins
as we forgive those who sin against us.
And do not bring us to the time of trial,
but deliver us from evil.

6 Thy kingdom come

We reflect on our longing for God's reign in our world

Singing

Keeping stillness Think of your life and your personality as territory. If there were flags to proclaim sovereignty over this territory, which sections would be under the banner of Christ, and which would have other flags, such as 'strictly private and personal', or 'unavailable for development'?

Leader There are places in our thinking and our loving where we have denied access to your reign in us.
Lord, have mercy.
Lord, have mercy.

There are sections of our behaviour where we turn your banners to face the other way.
Christ, have mercy.
Christ, have mercy.

There are pockets of resistance to your prompting, and determination to maintain our control.
Lord, have mercy.
Lord, have mercy.

Leader Father, give us the grace
to realign our longings with your longings,
our wills with your will,
and our vision of the kingdom with yours.

Singing

Keeping stillness Think over the situations and relationships you will be part of when you leave here, and during the coming week. Welcome God to reign in those places so that, when you come to them, the ground will already be God's territory.

All Our Father, who art in heaven,
hallowed be thy name.
Thy kingdom come.
Thy will be done on earth as it is in heaven.
Give us this day our daily bread
and forgive us our trespasses
as we forgive those who trespass against us.
Lead us not into temptation
but deliver us from evil.
For thine is the kingdom, the power and the glory
for ever and ever.
Amen.

Leader 'Do not be overcome by evil but overcome evil with good.'
All Amen. Let God's kingdom come.

Kevin Mayhew

All Father, let your kingdom come.
Reign in the whole of us
and in the whole of our life.
Amen.

Leader In this reading from the prophet Habakkuk, hear the vision of complete saturation of the world in the glory of God.

Reading Habakkuk 2:2-5

This is the word of the Lord.
Thanks be to God.

Leader Now hear how the full authority of Jesus' reign over the powers of darkness is recognised by the Roman centurion, using the experience of his own temporal authority.

Reading Matthew 8:5-13

This is the word of the Lord.
Thanks be to God.

Leader So we pray for those in positions of authority and responsibility, particularly wherever difficult and painful decisions have to be made.
Our Father in heaven:
let your kingdom come.

We pray for those elected to represent others
in places of government;
that your values and the example and life of Jesus
may guide their thinking and action.
Our Father in heaven:
let your kingdom come.

We pray for all monarchs
born into the responsibility of leadership.
Give them the grace and courage
to carry out their work in humility and integrity.
Our Father in heaven:
let your kingdom come.

Recognising the inherent dangers of corruption
wherever there is power,
we pray for all those with power
and influence internationally, nationally, locally
and in each home.
May they be constantly reminded of vigilance;
may they stand firm
against temptation to greed and self-indulgence,
pride, and insulation from those they serve.
Our Father in heaven:
let your kingdom come.

We pray for all who suffer
under repressive and corrupt regimes.
We stand alongside the oppressed
in their despair and silenced protest,
and pray for your justice and liberation
from all that crushes, marginalises and destroys.
Our Father in heaven:
let your kingdom come.

We thank you, heavenly Father,
for every person who has your kingdom reigning in their heart;
for all in whom your love and goodness is quietly growing;
for all whose lives you are currently transforming;
for all in whom the power of evil is being trampled underfoot.
Bless and water this growth of your kingdom.
Amen.

7 Thy will be done

*We reflect on the need for our wills to be
in harmony with the will of God*

Singing

A Even if it means shouldering a cross,
All your will, Lord, not ours be done.

Singing

All Our Father in heaven,
hallowed be your name.
Your kingdom come.
Your will be done on earth as in heaven.
Give us today our daily bread
and forgive us our sins
as we forgive those who sin against us.
Do not bring us to the time of trial
but deliver us from evil.
For the kingdom, the power and the glory
are yours for ever and ever.
Amen.

Leader Jesus said, 'Whoever does the will of my Father in heaven
is my brother and sister and mother.' *(Matthew 12:50)*

A But what is the will of God?

B And how are we to know?

Leader Jesus said, 'You shall love the Lord your God
with all your heart, and with all your mind,
and with all your strength.
You shall love your neighbour as yourself.' *(Mark 12:30-31)*

All Heavenly Father,
guide our minds and hearts as we contemplate your will.

Leader Jesus said, 'Remember, I am with you always,
to the end of the age.'

All Thanks be to God.

*Keeping
in
stillness* We are using this time of silence to contemplate together, in
the company of God, the love principle which underpins God's
will. Read slowly the words above (Mark 12:30-31) and let
God reveal to you what this means in practical terms for all of
us living in the world at the moment. Think of its implications
for individuals, communities, societies, nations and the Church.

Leader Hear the words of the prophet Micah, spelling out what it
means to live in tune with God's will.

Reading Micah 6:8

This is the word of the Lord.
Thanks be to God.

Leader Heavenly Father,
our will is so often at variance with yours,
our motives jar with your integrity,
our voiced intentions do not match with the way
we actually behave.

All Lord, have mercy on us and forgive us.

Leader Hear these words of encouragement. It is Jesus' concern never to discard, but always to gather up and restore.

Reading John 6:12, 38–39

This is the word of the Lord.
Thanks be to God.

Leader Though we have sinned, and rejected or ignored your will,
yet you desire that nothing and no one be lost.
It is your will to search out those who have drifted far from you,
and bring them safely home.

All Lord, have mercy on us and forgive us.

Leader The leper came to Jesus and said, 'If you are willing you can make me clean.' Jesus replied, 'I am willing; be clean.'

This is the saving word of the Lord.
Thanks be to God.

Singing

(Take a small piece of clay or dough.)

Keeping stillness As you shape and reshape the dough or clay in your hand, think of yourself as clay in the hands of God, the Potter, working with you in your life and circumstances, and carefully forming you. Allow yourself to trust God enough to let him make you into the person you were born to be, healing all that prevents this, and transforming all your past experiences, even the bad ones, into gifts of great value.

Press the clay or dough into the palm of your hand so that it takes on the shapes and patterns of your skin. Your life, being moulded in the palm of God's hand, will also take on his character.

(Place your piece of clay or dough by the worship focus.)

Leader O Lord, you are our Father;
All we are the clay, and you are our potter;
we are all the work of your hand.
(Isaiah 64:8)

Leader May we learn to desire what you desire;
All your will, Lord, not ours be done.
A In every conversation and every situation,
All your will, Lord, not ours be done.
B In all the choices and opportunities,
All your will, Lord, not ours be done.
A In the rocky places where your will looks hard,
All your will, Lord, not ours be done.
B Even if sacrifices have to be made,
All your will, Lord, not ours be done.

8 On earth as it is in heaven

*We reflect on the goodness of creation
and the needs of our world*

Singing

Leader God saw everything that he had made

All and indeed it was very good.

A Light and darkness,

B water and sky,

A dry land and vegetation,

B sun, moon and stars,

A sea creatures and birds,

B animals, insects and humans.

Leader God saw everything that he had made

All and indeed it was very good!

*Keeping
stillness* Using the worship focus to help you, and the words above, spend some time sharing God's joy at the goodness of creation. Imagine seeing it all for the first time, and allow yourself to wonder and delight in the gifts of nature we mostly take for granted.

Leader Holy . . . holy . . . holy . . .

All Holy . . . holy . . . holy . . .
Lord God of hosts.

Leader Give us this day our daily bread

All and forgive us our trespasses
as we forgive those who trespass against us.
Lead us not into temptation
but deliver us from evil.
For thine is the kingdom, the power and the glory
for ever and ever.
Amen.

Leader Protect us, O God, for in you we take refuge.

All You show us the path of life.

Leader In your presence there is fullness of joy;

All in your right hand are pleasures for evermore.
Amen.
(Psalm 16)

Leader Heaven and earth are full of your glory.

All Heaven and earth are full of your glory.
Glory be to you, O Lord most high.

Leader Hear these words from the book of Job, where God answers Job by directing him to see the awesome holiness of God through the wonders of creation.

Reading Job 38:1-18

This is the word of the Lord
Thanks be to God.

Leader Father in heaven, we give you thanks and praise

All for all the wonders of creation,
of which we ourselves are part.

A For colour and texture, light and shadow;

B for sounds, smells and tastes;

A for the laws of physics and chemistry;

B for intelligence to think with
and language to express our thoughts;

A for personalities and emotions to feel with
and respond to one another and to you;

B for the rich variety of climate, landscape and vegetation,
and all living creatures.

All Father in heaven, we give you thanks and praise.

Singing

Keeping stillness Bring to mind the areas where there is discord between God's good creation and our stewardship of the earth we have been given to live in.

Leader Our Father

All who art in heaven,
hallowed be your name.
May your kingdom come.

Leader Father, may your will be done

All on earth as it is in heaven.

Leader Wherever greed or arrogance crash in
where angels fear to tread . . . .
Father, may your will be done

All on earth as it is in heaven.

Leader Wherever destructive policies rule unchallenged . . . .
Father, may your will be done

All on earth as it is in heaven.

Leader When unjust distribution of wealth
leaves some complacent and most in poverty . . . .
Father, let your will be done

All on earth as it is in heaven.

Leader When resources are squandered
through short-term objectives . . . .
Father, let your will be done

All on earth as it is in heaven.

Leader When war and violence, poverty and oppression
make many into homeless refugees . . . .
Father, let your will be done

All on earth as it is in heaven.

9 Give us this day our daily bread

We reflect on our dependence on God for life, and our responsibility to share his gifts

Singing

Leader You, Father, are the Creator

All and we the children of your creative love.

Leader You, Father, are the Provider

All and we the receivers of your gifts.

Leader Yours, Lord, is the greatness, the splendour and the majesty.

All For all things come from you and of your own do we give you.

Keeping stillness Make your body still. Become aware of your breathing, and feel your pulse beating, keeping you alive. This life you have is a gift, given to you and sustained by God's love. Remind yourself of your complete dependence on God for life, and therefore all your daily needs. Wealth and temporal power lull us into thinking that we are really in control. Use this time to touch base with the deeper, hidden reality: we only exist and have free will to choose because God loves us and desires it for us. When we ask God to 'give us . . .' we are acknowledging our dependence on our Creator, and our trust in God as the Good Provider.

All Our Father, our loving parent, our Maker, our friend,
your very name is holy.
With the angels and saints we worship you.
As you reign in heaven,
so may the kingdom of heaven extend to all the earth.
As your will is accomplished in heaven,
so may your will be done on earth.
As your created beings, we trust in your good provision.
We ask for enough to enable us to live this day
in your love and service.
We commend to you the practical needs of us all.
We ask you to forgive us,
just as we have forgiven those who have offended us in any way.
Give us your protection against evil
and guide us away from temptation
so that we do not fall into sin.
We pray these things to you alone
because the kingdom is yours,
and all power and glory are yours,
for ever and for ever.
Amen.

Leader As God our Provider teaches us,
may we live generously, take joy in giving,
and share whatever we have with one another.

All For in God alone is our treasure and our security.
Amen.

Kevin Mayhew

Leader Hear these words of Jesus, as he teaches his followers about God's loving, daily provision.

Reading Luke 12:22-31

This is the word of the Lord.
Thanks be to God.

Singing

Leader Blessed be God our Father,
All who gives good gifts to his children.
Men The sun shines on both unjust and just.
Women The rain falls on both evil and good.
Leader Blessed be God our Father,
All who gives good gifts to his children.

Women Perfectly and finely tuned,
this planet supports life in diversity and abundance.

Men Perfectly and finely tuned,
the universe is governed by laws which anchor,
yet allow for development and change.

Leader Blessed be God our Father,
All who gives good gifts to his children.
Men Though the gifts are taken while the Giver is ignored;
Women though demands are made which conflict with his will;
Leader blessed be God our Father,
All who gives good gifts to his children.

Leader The Lord is your keeper;
All the Lord is your shade at your right hand.

Leader The sun shall not strike you by day,
All nor the moon by night.
Leader The Lord will keep you from all evil;
All he will keep your life.
Leader Blessed be God our Father,
All who gives good gifts to his children.
Leader Let us open our hearts and minds
to the gifts God wants to give us.
(From Psalm 121)

Keeping stillness Trusting our heavenly Father, we are going to use this space to receive from God not what we have decided we would like, but what God wishes to give us, both as individuals and as Church. We do this by faith, not sight, because the gifts may be given without any outward sign. We do it thankfully, happy to receive whatever strength or protection, healing or anointing God needs us to have, whether it matches our plans or not.

Singing

Keeping stillness In your imagination, gather around you those you long to know God as the giver of good gifts: those who at present do not trust him, or do not know him as he really is; those who need to know they are loved, accepted and forgiven; those who are trying to live good lives in their own strength. Imagine yourself distributing God's love to them from the huge, limitless resources of God's abundance.

10 And forgive us our trespasses

We reflect on our need for forgiveness,
and on God's merciful love

As the candle is lit, say together:

All Your light, O God, shines in the darkness
and the darkness does not quench it. *(John 1)*
Shine in our darkness, heavenly Father,
so that we may see more clearly
where our sin obstructs your love,
and denies you entrance to our lives
and residence in our hearts and minds.
Amen.

Leader Love is patient; love is kind;

All love is patient; love is kind;

Leader love is not envious, or boastful or arrogant or rude.

All love is not envious, or boastful or arrogant or rude.

Leader It does not insist on its own way;

All it does not insist on its own way;

Leader it is not irritable or resentful;

All it is not irritable or resentful;

Leader it does not rejoice in wrongdoing, but rejoices in the truth.

All it does not rejoice in wrongdoing, but rejoices in the truth.

Leader It bears all things,

All believes all things,

Leader hopes all things,

All endures all things.

Keep us in your love for ever,
protect us from all that is evil,
within and without,
and help us to walk in step with you,
neither dragging behind nor racing ahead
but in your close company
for the rest of our life.
Amen.

Leader May God, who alone can forgive our sin,
take from us all that is evil,
so that we can start again.
And may he refresh us daily as we travel.
Amen.

Leader This is the word of the Lord.

All Thanks be to God.

(1 Corinthians 13:4-7)

Keeping stillness Use this time to work slowly through the passage from Corinthians, substituting first the name of Jesus, and then, in the echo, your own name. You will find this will help you notice the areas of sinfulness in your living which are not 'misdemeanours' but orientation to self rather than love.

Leader Hear Luke's account of Jesus giving the deep healing and freeing of God's forgiveness to a paralysed man.

Reading Luke 5:17-26

This is the word of the Lord.

Thanks be to God.

Singing

Keeping stillness Spend this time naming to God, your heavenly Father, the thoughts, speech, actions and missed opportunities for loving service which grieve his heart of love. Name them, neither making excuses nor shouldering blame which is not yours. Name and confess them simply out of a longing to put things right with God, and steer a new course, in the wake of his forgiveness.

Leader Heavenly Father, calling to mind the pain our lack of love causes you,

All we long for your forgiveness.

Leader Calling to mind the sadness and heartache we have caused others,

All we long for your forgiveness.

Leader Calling to mind the opportunities for love and generosity which we have missed or avoided,

All we long for your forgiveness.

Leader Calling to mind the righteousness we have despised and the justice we have failed to uphold or protect,

All we long for your forgiveness.

Leader Lord . . . have mercy.

All Lord . . . have mercy.

Leader Christ . . . have mercy.

All Christ . . . have mercy.

Leader Lord . . . have mercy.

All Lord . . . have mercy.

As an outward sign of this cleansing, wash your hands in the water and allow someone else to dry them. Music can be sung or played during this time.

Leader Like water flowing in the parched desert

All your forgiveness cleanses, refreshes and revives.

Leader Like gentle summer rain falling after a drought

All your forgiveness cleanses, refreshes and revives.

Leader Like bathing or showering after a hard day at work

All your forgiveness cleanses, refreshes and revives.

Leader Heavenly Father,

All it is your loving acceptance which sets us free, lightens our hearts and fills us with your joy.

11 As we forgive those who trespass against us

We reflect on the freedom forgiveness offers, and our commission to set others free

Singing

Leader Jesus said, 'For if you forgive others their trespasses, your heavenly Father will also forgive you, but if you do not forgive others, neither will your Father forgive your trespasses.' *(Matthew 6:14-15)*

While half of you follow the Stillness exercise, the others will be praying for you. After a few minutes, swap roles.

Keeping This is one of the hard sayings of Jesus, but he is very clear
stillness and firm on the necessity for forgiving others. Let its significance and its implications sink in as you run your memory over your life and notice the patches where you have not yet managed to forgive completely, or where you are still holding out against forgiveness. These are bound to be the raw places where you still hurt, so you are being upheld and supported by the prayers of those around you. Don't do anything with these areas yet – just recognise and acknowledge them in Jesus' presence.

Provide for us our daily needs
and forgive us our sin
as we have forgiven those who sin against us.
Do not lead us into temptation
but set us free from evil.
For the kingdom, all power and all glory
belong to you for ever and ever.
Amen.

Singing

Leader Will you take Christ's love out into the world?
All In the power of Christ, we will.

Leader Will you walk the way of mercy and forgiveness?
All In the life of Christ, we will.

Leader Will you build one another up in faith and love?
All With the grace of Christ, we will.
Amen.

Leader 'For if you forgive others their trespasses, your heavenly Father will also forgive you, but if you do not forgive others, neither will your Father forgive your trespasses.'
(*Matthew 6:14-15*)

All Father, you love and accept us,
in spite of our weak and fitful love for you.
Give us the grace to forgive others,
however much and however often
they have trespassed against us.
And wherever the hurt to us or to those we love
makes it particularly hard to forgive,
then pour into our hearts
more and more of your love and mercy
until we are able to forgive and set our enemies free.
Amen.

Leader Hear the hard and challenging words of Jesus on the difficult task of forgiving others.

Reading Matthew 18:21-35

This is the word of the Lord.
Thanks be to God.

Leader God's forgiveness of us depends on our forgiveness of others. There is no way round it.

Men No way to avoid it; no use ignoring it.

Women No point in pretending it's done, when the bitterness still lingers.

All God's forgiveness of us depends on our forgiveness of others.

Leader If we say we have forgiven

Women but the offences are stored up for use in later arguments,

All then we still have some forgiving to do.

Leader If we say we have forgiven

Men but we continue to tell the story of past wrongs,

All then we still have some forgiving to do.

Leader If we say we have forgiven

All but the present is still driven by the past,
then we still have some forgiving to do.
Father of mercy, give us the grace to forgive.

Singing

Keeping stillness God's grace is here in abundance for you to use. As he pours his love into your heart, be more generous in your forgiveness than you have ever been before. Reaffirm your forgiveness of situations and people you thought you had already forgiven years ago. Thank God for empowering you to forgive, setting others free.

Leader Heavenly Father, we give you thanks and praise for the cleansing and healing of old and festering wounds; for the liberating power of forgiveness, both for others and for ourselves as we forgive.

All Blessed be God for ever.
Amen.

Leader As Jesus teaches us, so let us pray.

All Abba, Father, Holy One,
let your kingdom and your will be accomplished here on earth as in your heaven.

12 Lead us not into temptation

We reflect on the power of temptation,
and our urgent need to watch and pray

Leader Jesus said, 'Stay awake and pray that you may not come into the time of temptation and trial.'
(Matthew 26:41)

Singing

Leader Hear again the familiar words from Genesis, noticing the path from temptation to sin.

Reading Genesis 4:1-10

This is the word of the Lord.
Thanks be to God.

Keeping stillness Think over the situations which you have found from experience are particular areas of temptation for you. They may be linked with circumstances you cannot avoid. They may be linked to physical weakness or emotional scar tissue, genes or upbringing. Recognise where you are now, not where you might be if things had been different. And know that your heavenly Father has the knowledge and power to lead you safely through the minefields of temptation. Commit yourself to his guidance, trusting him and ready to act on his leadership.

those who make themselves available
and are ready to listen and stand alongside.
Amen.

Keeping stillness Thank God for those who have helped or encouraged you, or enabled you to avoid falling into temptation.

All Father in heaven
whose name is holy,
may your kingdom be established on earth as in heaven.
May your will be chosen and accomplished
on earth as in heaven.
On you we depend for the gift of life and our daily sustaining.
Give us what we need and take from us our sin.
Do not lead us into temptation but set us free from evil.
We pray to you in the knowledge
that the kingdom is yours alone;
all power and glory are yours now and for ever.
Amen.

Singing

Leader The Lord will keep you from all evil;
All he will keep your life.
Leader The Lord will keep your going out and your coming in
All from this time on and for evermore.
Amen.
(Psalm 121)

Kevin Mayhew

Leader As we prepare ourselves by watchfulness and prayer,
we call to mind all those
who are vulnerable to temptation at the moment;
those who are cut off from their usual support
and encouragement.
Father,
lead them not into temptation.

For those whose addiction is screaming;
whose anger is close to explosion;
whose debt nags and threatens;
whose desires whine.
Father,
lead them not into temptation.

We pray for those who have grown complacent
about the dangers of temptation,
or arrogant about their ability to resist.
We pray for those excited by evil and seeking it out.
Father,
lead them not into temptation.

We pray for all who entice others into temptation;
those who encourage addiction and play on people's needs;
those who profit from others' weakness or financial mistakes.
Father,
lead them not into temptation.

We pray for those who are dispirited after previous failures
and have little energy for continuing the fight against sin;
for those whose past sins stare back from the mirror
and cancel good intentions.
Father,
lead them not into temptation.

We thank you for all who work to encourage
and strengthen others in their battle against temptation;

Leader Even before we were born

All God saw us, knew us and loved us.

Leader Through every stage of our growing

All God saw us, knew us and loved us.

Leader Whenever we fought valiantly against evil,
and whenever we fell into temptation

All God saw us, knew us and loved us.

Leader When we lost our way and when we were oppressed,
when we were ashamed and full of guilt

All God saw us, knew us and loved us.

Leader For, like us, Jesus was tempted,
and understood temptation's power.

All Like us, he was faced with difficult decisions.

Leader The cross displays the sacrifice he made,

All and by his wounds we are healed.

Singing

Keeping stillness During this time ask God to strengthen your will to remain faithful
for the times of temptation ahead, and to heal those areas which
make you particularly prone to temptation.

Leader Father, we thank you for your empowering.
We thank you that you know us completely,
understand our areas of weakness,
and walk with us through the valleys of darkness.

All In the shadow of your wings I will take refuge,
until the destroying storms pass by.
(*Psalm 57*)

13 But deliver us from evil

We reflect on God's power to save and rescue us

and are carrying heavy burdens,
and I will give you rest.
Take my yoke upon you, and learn from me;
for I am gentle and humble in heart,
and you will find rest for your souls.
For my yoke is easy, and my burden is light.'
(Matthew 11:28-29)

Leader Whenever the darkness of evil shocks us
with its terrifying power,

All give us your light to banish the dark.

Leader Whenever evil distorts truth, undermines goodness,
corrupts or destroys,

All give us the courage to stand firm in the power of love
so that we shall not be shaken.
Let the kingdom come!
Let the will of God be done!
Let evil perish!
Amen.

Singing

Leader Be still.

All Be still and know that I am God.

Keeping stillness Just as still water reflects faithfully, so in this stillness let God's love and goodness be reflected in the still water of your soul at rest in his company.

Leader Then I heard every creature in heaven and on earth and under the earth and in the sea, and all that is in them, singing,

All 'To the one seated on the throne and to the Lamb
be blessing and honour and glory and might
for ever and ever!'
(Revelation 5:13)

Leader As the waters cover the sea

All so may the whole earth be filled with the glory of God.

Leader As salt without taste is trampled underfoot

All so may the powers of darkness be crushed beneath our feet.

Leader May the love and goodness of God reign in every heart and mind.

All May all that is good and lovely, faithful and true be safely gathered in, so that nothing is lost.

Singing

Leader The Lord is faithful.

All He will strengthen us and guard us from evil.

Leader The Lord is always with us

All even to the end of time.

Leader Give thanks to the Lord for he is good.

All His steadfast love endures for ever.
Amen.

Leader May we be delivered from all evil, without and within.

All May we be set free from all that is offensive to the one true God, Father, Son and Holy Spirit.

Leader Hear these two readings which tell of the God who saves us.

Reading Exodus 3:4-8a

Leader God promised to set his people free from the slavery of Egypt.

All Blessed be God who rescues and redeems us.

Reading Matthew 26:26-28

Leader God promises to set his people free from the slavery of sin.

All Blessed be God who rescues and redeems us.

Keeping stillness Let God deliver you from evil, without and within. He can free you from being a slave to any area of sin, however ingrained it feels. He can free you from the tyranny of any obsessive yearnings, destructive tendencies or buried fears. He can show you the way out of any prison of guilt, hatred or jealousy which holds you in its grip. Let him rescue you and open the doors to a new freedom.

Leader God promises to set his people free:

All free to worship him without fear all the days of their life.

Singing

Leader Let us pray for all who suffer tyranny and oppression, whether under corrupt government or behind closed doors in the family home. Father,

deliver us from evil.

We remember all for whom peace is fragile, volatile and uneasy; all who must be constantly vigilant and guarded in their speech for fear of reprisals to them or their loved ones. Father,

deliver us from evil.

We pray for all who live in a climate of fear or ridicule; all who are starting to believe the lies against them. Father,

deliver us from evil.

We pray for those driven to seek asylum far from home and family, and all who struggle for justice in the face of contempt or hostility. Father,

deliver us from evil.

Keeping stillness In this space of stillness, stand alongside those who have no voice, but whose lives are crippled or blighted by the evil they face each day. Feel with the vulnerable and the desperate, and bring their pain into the presence of God.

Leader Jesus said,

All 'Come to me, all you that are weary

14 For thine is the kingdom, the power and the glory

We reflect on getting our priorities right

Keeping stillness Jesus often spoke of the hidden growth of the kingdom, starting small, like yeast or mustard seed, but with enormous potential for great effect. In this space, as we honour God, think first of yourself, and then of your church, as dough which God's yeast is in the process of transforming. Thank God for this hidden work, and pray for the yeast of the kingdom to work its way through-out the whole of the dough, so that the world can be fed.

All Holy God, Abba, Father,
reign in our lives as King.
Let our wills be at one with yours.
Give us daily bread. Take from us our sin.
Teach us to forgive.
Alert us to temptation. Guard us from evil.
To the Keeper of the kingdom we pray.
To the One with lasting power and glory we pray.
You, our Father, we worship
now and in eternity.
Amen.

Singing

Leader Then David blessed the Lord in the presence of all the assembly; David said:

All Blessed are you, O Lord, the God of our ancestor Israel, for ever and ever. Yours, O Lord, are the greatness, the power, the glory, the victory, and the majesty; for all that is in the heavens and on the earth is yours; yours is the kingdom, O Lord, and you are exalted above all.

Leader Riches and honour come from you, and you rule over all.

All In your hand are power and might; and it is in your hand to make great and to give strength to all.

Leader And now, our God, we give thanks to you

All and praise your glorious name.
Amen.
(1 Chronicles 29:10-13)

Singing

Leader Blessed be the Lord, the God of Israel,
from everlasting to everlasting.
And let all the people say,

All 'Amen. Praise the Lord.'

Singing

Keeping stillness Slowly and imaginatively, work your way through the words of King David's prayer, thinking of the different land, sky and seascapes of God's awesome creation, and the experience you have of God orchestrating good in the face of evil. Think of yourself as a musical instrument on which the song of God's praise is played, through the Spirit within you.

Kevin
Mayhew

Leader All too often we snatch at the kingdom, coveting the power and glory for ourselves.

All But today we commit ourselves to giving God the glory.

Leader All too often we create around us a world on which we can stamp our will and our control.

All But today we commit ourselves to giving God the glory.

Leader All too often, by careful editing, we pocket the credit which rightly belongs to God.

All But today we commit ourselves to giving God the glory.

All glory be to the one true God,
who is Father, Son and Holy Spirit;
as God was in the beginning,
is now, as we speak,
and will always be
for ever. Amen.

Singing

Leader As you hear the psalmist's words of praise, let the praises resonate in your own heart and soul, so that they become your own act of worship.

Reading Psalm 104:1-33

This is the word of the Lord.
Thanks be to God.

Keeping stillness Recognising that the kingdom, power and glory belong to God means relinquishing our eagerness to control, and voluntarily working co-operatively with God instead, even if the workplace and task may surprise us, and his priorities differ from our own. In this space, offer yourself to be available for the work of the kingdom on God's terms. As our desires become yoked to God's will, so we will be increasingly able to share in the work of the kingdom.

Leader Let us pray for the Church of Christ, that it may truly reveal God's kingdom, power and glory on earth.
Not to us,
but to you be the glory, Lord God.

For fresh courage to look candidly at our discipleship and welcome God's whispered advice.
Not to us,
but to you be the glory, Lord God.

For an amnesty of ambitious agendas and empire-building, and an eagerness instead to cultivate the fruits of the Spirit.
Not to us,
but to you be the glory, Lord God.

For the grace to travel lightly, live simply and take stewardship seriously.
Not to us,
but to you be the glory, Lord God.

For the humility to be body parts, celebrating our membership of the worldwide Body of Christ.
Not to us,
but to you be the glory, Lord God.

For a more urgent thirst for righteousness and justice, for fervent prayer, and a willingness to be a part of the solution.
Not to us,
but to you be the glory, Lord God.

For closer attentiveness to God, wider compassion, deeper faith, and greater love.
Not to us,
but to you be the glory, Lord God.
For the kingdom, the power and the glory are yours for ever and ever. Amen.

May your feeding and forgiveness
be mirrored in our lives.
Protect us in temptation and shield us from evil.
Your kingdom lasts for ever and ever;
your power and glory never fail.
Alleluia. Amen.

Leader Heavenly Father, we give you thanks and praise
for all those through whom the message of your love
has been brought down to us.

Men For those who battled with danger and death
to keep the flame alive and deliver it on to others.

Women For those who through the generations
reflected on your love and shared what they had learnt.

Men For grandparents, parents, children and grandchildren
catching the story and passing it faithfully on.

Women For pastors and teachers,
and all whose lives have been dedicated
to the spread of your gospel and strengthening faith.

Men For all who are working now
to reach those who do not know you
and dare not trust your love.

Leader For all who have taught us by their example,
made us think, allowed us to doubt,
and loved us into the kingdom,

All heavenly Father, we give you thanks and praise.
May the story continue to be told.
May the flame of your love burn bright in our lives
and may our children's children live to praise your name. Amen.

15 For ever and ever

*We reflect on the nature of eternity and
the eternally present*

Leader For ever and ever God is,
and the things of God hold true.

All For ever and ever the kingdom stands, sunlit with love
and stretching into the distance of faithfulness.

Leader For ever and ever the Spirit broods,
breathes life and bears fruit.

All For ever and ever God is,
and the things of God hold true.

Singing

Keeping stillness With your finger, slowly trace round and round the knotwork
pattern, thinking as you do so: 'For ever and ever God is, and
the things of God hold true.' Let this pattern of movement and
thinking teach your soul and settle you in the ordered love of
his Being.

Leader As time dwellers we come to visit eternity

All and discover not length of days
but a lasting presence of love.

Leader We find not sequence

All but orchestration.
Not 'before and after'

Leader but 'now'.

All May we not be distracted from this calling.

Leader Father, in all our future plans and decisions

All anoint our vision with your perception;
anoint our hearing with your understanding;
anoint our activity with your direction;
that we may share in your 'ever'
as we walk through the 'now',
our lives reflecting your love
and making you known. Amen.

Singing

Leader Hear the prophet Isaiah speaking out God's assurance to his people of ongoing strength and refreshment.

Reading Isaiah 40:27-31

This is the word of the Lord.
Thanks be to God.

Keeping stillness Welcome God's lasting kingdom into the different areas of your life and the life of your church. Imagine the meetings and activities, the in-tray, diary, financial reports and times of gathered prayer, committing it all to God's prioritising and in the context of God's kingdom values.

All Ever-present God, holy and loving,
your children come to pray your kingdom in.
May your reign and your will transform us all,
till heaven and earth are one.

All For ever and ever, O Lord, the kingdom is yours;
for ever and ever all power belongs to you;
for ever and ever your glory brightens heaven,
touching earth now with the warmth of hope,
and drawing us into your presence.

Leader Hear these words written to an early Christian community and to you, now, celebrating things of lasting significance.

Reading Colossians 1:3-20

This is the word of the Lord.
Thanks be to God.

Keeping stillness Use this time to consider yourself and your church as part of God's 'ever'. Think over the qualities which will last beyond death, and recognise what is only temporal. Notice any imbalance of priority in the way energy and resources are directed. Is too much time and money being spent on what is temporal, and not enough on what is eternal?

Leader Jesus said,
'Make purses for yourselves that do not wear out,
an unfailing treasure in heaven,
where no thief comes near and no moth destroys.

All 'For where your treasure is,
there your heart will be also.'

Leader St Paul wrote,
'And now faith, hope, and love abide, these three;

All 'and the greatest of these is love.'

Leader So, Father, give us the grace to seek as our priority
the kingdom of God and his righteousness.

16 Amen

We reflect on our committed response to the call of God

Singing

Leader Jesus said, 'You did not choose me but I chose you. And I appointed you to go and bear fruit, fruit that will last.'
(John 15:16)

Keeping stillness Let the significance of Jesus' words sink in. It is God's hand on your life which has drawn you here to be spending time in his company. It is his Spirit enabling you to pray. Keep your body still and attentive, giving God the chance to speak into your heart and mind of his love for you and his hopes for you.

Leader Father, let your will be done in us
All for you have the words of eternal life.
Leader Let your love take root in us
All for apart from you we can do nothing.
Leader Let your kingdom grow in us
All for your steadfast love is as high as the heavens; your faithfulness extends to the clouds.

Leader Hear this account of Isaiah's calling and commissioning, noticing the stages of listening and new insight, repentance, cleansing and self-offering.

All let God's kingdom come!
Women In hurt and hatred, ache and anger,
All let God's kingdom come!
All Our Father, our Parent, our great God of heaven, let your kingdom come.
Let your will be done in us and in all your people.
Sustain us and provide for us in all our needs.
Free us from our sin through your forgiveness, as we free others by our forgiveness.
Keep us from falling and save us from evil.
We pray in the sure knowledge that the power and glory of your reign lasts for ever and ever. Amen.

Keeping stillness In this time give thanks to God in faith for the growth of his kingdom in every act of love and compassion throughout the world, every unselfish thought and honest transaction, every seeking after truth and justice, goodness and humility.

Leader Finally, beloved, whatever is true, whatever is honourable, whatever is just, whatever is pure, whatever is pleasing, whatever is commendable, if there is any excellence and if there is anything worthy of praise, think about these things.

All Amen!
May our lives be transformed by the life of Christ within us. Amen.

Reading Isaiah 6:1-8

This is the word of the Lord.
Thanks be to God.

Keeping stillness God never sends us anywhere without equipping us for the task. He never asks of us what we cannot do. But it is never us working in our own strength for God; it is always collaborative ministry – working with God in his strength and in step with his timing. In the stillness, ask for God's grace to understand this and act on it.

Leader Hear now the calling and commissioning of Mary.

Reading Luke 1:26-38

This is the word of the Lord.
Thanks be to God.

Keeping stillness What God needed of Mary was not a total understanding of the task ahead, or of the reasons she had been chosen, but simply the willingness to say 'Yes' and go with God into the altered future, trusting him. Our 'Amen' to the Lord's Prayer is similar. It is our committed 'Yes' to God.

Singing

Leader Let us pray for one another, that we may be firm in purpose, flexible in God's hands and filled with his love.

Pray with one another in pairs and threes for particular tasks and God's anointing for them, for areas of difficulty or confusion about direction, and for God's blessing and guidance in ongoing work and ministry.

Leader Heavenly Father,
we think of all who pray as Jesus taught us,
and pray for them now.

Men The very young, who have just learnt to speak your name;

Women the very old and frail, their lips barely moving but their hearts full of a lifetime's trust;

Men the sound of many voices praying as one;

Women the tiny, scattered groups of people praying in mountain and desert, forest and at sea;

Men the hesitant prayers of those who are turning back to you at last;

Women the prayers of those imprisoned for their faith;

Men those unaccustomed but desperate, praying in the turmoil of disaster;

Women those in the freshness of new faith, and full of joy.

Leader As the planet turns, and shadows shrink and stretch the earth is circled by the voice of prayer:

All God's love and our response.

Leader Like the ice of winter melting into spring,

All let God's kingdom come!

Men Like welcome rain on the parched and thirsty ground,

All let God's kingdom come!

Women Like the strong, hidden growing of roots in the earth,

All let God's kingdom come!

Leader Like the fullgrown wheat for the feeding of many,

All let God's kingdom come!

Men In hearts and households, changes and choices,